SIDEWAYS STORIES FROM
WAYSIDE SCHOOL

LOUIS SACHAR

ILLUSTRATED BY TIM HEITZ

Long tail Books

In memory of Robert J. Sachar
and to my mother, Andy, and Jeff.

Sideways Stories from Wayside School
Text copyright © 1978 by Louis Sachar
Illustrations copyright © 2019 by Tim Heitz
All rights reserved.

ISBN 979-11-91343-01-4

Longtail Books

INTRODUCTION

This book **contains** thirty stories about the children and teachers at Wayside School. But before we get to them, there is something you **ought to** know so that you don't get **confused**.

Wayside School was **accidentally** built **sideways**.

It was supposed to be only one **story** high, with thirty classrooms all in a **row**. Instead it is thirty stories high, with one classroom on each story. The **builder** said he was very sorry.

The children at Wayside like having a sideways school. They have an **extra-large playground**.

The children and teachers **described** in this book all go to class on the top floor. So there are thirty stories from the thirtieth story of Wayside School.

It has been said that these stories are strange and **silly**. That is probably true. However, when I told stories about you to the children at Wayside, they thought you were strange and silly. That is probably also true.

1. MRS. GORF

Mrs. Gorf had a long **tongue** and **pointed** ears. She was the meanest teacher in Wayside School. She taught the class on the thirtieth **story**.

"If you children are bad," she **warn**ed, "or if you answer a problem wrong, I'll **wiggle** my ears, **stick out** my tongue, and **turn** you **into** apples!" Mrs. Gorf didn't like children, but she loved apples.

Joe couldn't add. He couldn't even **count**. But he knew that if he answered a problem wrong, he would be turned into an apple. So he copied from John. He didn't like to **cheat**, but Mrs.

Gorf had never taught him how to add.

One day Mrs. Gorf caught Joe copying John's paper. She wiggled her ears—first her right one, then her left—stuck out her tongue, and turned Joe into an apple. Then she turned John into an apple for letting Joe cheat.

"Hey, that isn't fair," said Todd. "John was only trying to help a friend."

Mrs. Gorf wiggled her ears—first her right one, then her left—stuck out her tongue, and turned Todd into an apple. "Does anybody else have an **opinion**?" she asked.

Nobody said a word.

Mrs. Gorf laughed and placed the three apples on her desk.

Stephen started to cry. He couldn't help it. He was **scare**d.

"I do not allow crying in the classroom," said Mrs. Gorf. She wiggled her ears—first her right one, then her left—stuck out her tongue, and turned Stephen into an apple.

For the rest of the day, the children were **absolute**ly quiet. And when they went home, they were too scared even to talk to their parents.

But Joe, John, Todd, and Stephen couldn't go home. Mrs. Gorf just left them on her desk. They were able to talk to each other, but they didn't have much to say.

Their parents were very worried. They didn't know where their children were. Nobody seemed to know.

The next day Kathy was late for school. As soon as she walked in, Mrs. Gorf turned her into an apple.

Paul **sneeze**d during class. He was turned into an apple.

Nancy said, "God **bless** you!" when Paul sneezed. Mrs. Gorf wiggled her ears—first her right one, then her left—stuck out her tongue, and turned Nancy into an apple.

Terrence fell out of his chair. He was turned into an apple.

Maurecia tried to **run away**. She was **halfway** to the door as Mrs. Gorf's right ear began to wiggle. When she reached the door, Mrs. Gorf's left ear wiggled. Maurecia opened the door and had one foot outside when Mrs. Gorf stuck out her tongue. Maurecia became an apple.

Mrs. Gorf picked up the apple from the floor and put it on her desk with the others. Then a funny thing happened. Mrs. Gorf turned around and fell over a piece of **chalk**.

The three Erics laughed. They were turned into apples.

Mrs. Gorf had a **dozen** apples on her desk: Joe, John, Todd, Stephen, Kathy, Paul, Nancy, Terrence, Maurecia, and the three Erics—Eric Fry, Eric Bacon, and Eric Ovens.

Louis, the **yard** teacher, walked into the classroom. He had missed the children at **recess**. He had heard that Mrs. Gorf was a mean teacher. So he came up to **investigate**. He saw the twelve apples on Mrs. Gorf's desk. "I must be wrong," he thought. "She must be a good teacher if so many children bring her apples." He walked back down to the **playground**.

The next day a dozen more children were turned into apples.

Louis, the yard teacher, came back into the room. He saw twenty-four apples on Mrs. Gorf's desk. There were only three children left in the class. "She must be the best teacher in the world," he thought.

By the end of the week all of the children were apples. Mrs. Gorf was very happy. "Now I can go home," she said. "I don't have to teach anymore. I won't have to walk up thirty **flights of stairs** ever again."

"You're not going anywhere," shouted Todd. He jumped off the desk and **bop**ped Mrs. Gorf on the nose. The rest of the apples followed. Mrs. Gorf fell on the floor. The apples jumped all over her.

"Stop," she shouted, "or I'll turn you into applesauce!"

But the apples didn't stop, and Mrs. Gorf could do nothing about it.

"Turn us back into children," Todd **demand**ed.

Mrs. Gorf had no choice. She stuck out her tongue, wiggled her ears—this time her left one first, then her right—and turned the apples back into children.

"All right," said Maurecia, "let's go get Louis. He'll know what to do."

"No!" **scream**ed Mrs. Gorf. "I'll turn you back into apples." She wiggled her ears—first her right one, then her left—and stuck out her tongue. But Jenny held up a mirror, and Mrs. Gorf turned herself into an apple.

The children didn't know what to do. They didn't have a teacher. Even though Mrs. Gorf was mean, they didn't think it was right to leave her as an apple. But none of them knew how to wiggle their ears.

Louis, the yard teacher, walked in. "Where's Mrs. Gorf?" he asked.

Nobody said a word.

"Boy,[1] am I hungry," said Louis. "I don't think Mrs. Gorf would mind if I ate this apple. **After all**, she always has so many."

He picked up the apple, which was really Mrs. Gorf, shined it up on his shirt, and ate it.

---

1 boy 소년이나 남자아이를 나타내는 명사가 아니라, 놀람이나 기쁨을 나타내는 감탄사로 '어머나' 혹은 '맙소사'라는 의미이다.

2. MRS. JEWLS

Mrs. Jewls had a **terribly** nice face. She stood at the bottom of Wayside School and looked up. She was supposed to teach the class on the thirtieth story.

The children on the thirtieth story were **scared**. They had never told anybody what had happened to Mrs. Gorf. They hadn't had a teacher for three days. They were afraid of what their new teacher would be like. They had heard she'd be a terribly nice teacher. They had never had a nice teacher. They were terribly afraid of nice teachers.

Mrs. Jewls walked up the **wind**ing, **creak**ing **staircase** to the thirtieth story. She was also afraid. She was afraid of the children. She had heard that they would be **horribly** cute children. She had never taught cute children. She was horribly afraid of cute children.

She opened the door to the classroom. She was terribly nice. The children could tell just by looking at her.

Mrs. Jewls looked at the children. They were horribly cute. In fact, they were much too cute to be children.

"I don't believe it," said Mrs. Jewls. "It's a room full of monkeys!"

The children looked at each other. They didn't see any monkeys.

"This is **ridiculous**," said Mrs. Jewls, "just ridiculous. I walked **all the way** up thirty **flights of stairs** for nothing but a class of monkeys. What do they think I am? I'm a teacher, not a **zookeeper!**"

The children looked at her. They didn't know what to say. Todd **scratch**ed his head.

"Oh, I'm sorry," said Mrs. Jewls. "Please don't **get** me **wrong**. I have nothing against monkeys. It is just that I was **expect**ing children. I like monkeys. I really do. Why,[1] I'm sure we can play all kinds of monkey games."

"What are you talking about?" asked Todd.

Mrs. Jewls nearly fell off her chair. "Well, what do you know, a talking monkey. Tomorrow I'll bring you a banana."

"My name is Todd," said Todd.

---

1 why 이유를 묻거나 말할 때 쓰는 의문사 또는 관계사가 아닌 '어머', '아니'라는 뜻의 감탄사로 쓰였다.

The children were **flabbergasted**. They all raised their hands.

"I'm sorry," said Mrs. Jewls, "but I don't have enough bananas for all of you. I didn't expect this. Next week I'll bring in a whole bushel.²"

"I don't want a banana," said Calvin. "I'm not a monkey."

"Would you like a peanut?" asked Mrs. Jewls. "I think I might have a bag of peanuts in my **purse**. Wait a second. Yes, here it is."

"Thanks," said Calvin. Calvin liked peanuts.

Allison stood up. "I'm not a monkey," she said. "I'm a girl. My name is Allison. And so is everybody else."

Mrs. Jewls was shocked. "Do you mean to tell me that every monkey in here is named Allison?"

"No," said Jenny. "She means we are all children. My name is Jenny."

"No," said Mrs. Jewls. "You're much too cute to be children."

Jason raised his hand.

"Yes," said Mrs. Jewls, "the chimpanzee³ in the red shirt."

"My name is Jason," said Jason, "and I'm not a chimpanzee."

"You're too small to be a gorilla,⁴" said Mrs. Jewls.

"I'm a boy," said Jason.

"You're not a monkey?" asked Mrs. Jewls.

---

2 bushel 곡물이나 과일의 중량 단위인 부셸. 1부셸은 8갤런(약 30리터)이다.
3 chimpanzee 침팬지. 크기는 1미터에서 1.7미터 정도이고 다리보다 팔이 길고 손이 긴 유인원.
4 gorilla 고릴라. 영장목 중 가장 큰 종으로 크기는 1.5미터에서 1.9미터 정도이다.

"No," said Jason.

"And the rest of the class, they're not monkeys, either?" asked Mrs. Jewls.

"No," said Allison. "That is what we've been trying to tell you."

"Are you sure?" asked Mrs. Jewls.

"We'd know if we were monkeys, wouldn't we?" asked Calvin.

"I don't know," said Mrs. Jewls. "Do monkeys know that they are monkeys?"

"I don't know," said Allison. "I'm not a monkey."

"No, I suppose you're not," said Mrs. Jewls. "Okay, in that case, we have a lot of work to do—reading, writing, **subtract**ion, addition, **spell**ing. Everybody take out a piece of paper. We will have a test now."

Jason **tap**ped Todd on the shoulder. He said, "Do you want to know something? I liked it better when she thought we were monkeys."

"I know," said Todd. "I guess now it means she won't bring me a banana."

"There will be no talking in class," said Mrs. Jewls. She wrote Todd's name on the **blackboard** under the word **DISCIPLINE**.

12

3. JOE

Joe had **curly** hair. But he didn't know how much hair he had. He couldn't **count** that high. In fact, he couldn't count at all.

When all of the other children went to **recess**, Mrs. Jewls told Joe to wait inside. "Joe," she said. "How much hair do you have?"

Joe **shrug**ged his shoulders. "A lot," he answered.

"But how much, Joe?" asked Mrs. Jewls.

"Enough to **cover** my head," Joe answered.

"Joe, you are going to have to learn how to count," said Mrs. Jewls.

"But, Mrs. Jewls, I already know how to count," said Joe. "Let me go to recess."

"First count to ten," said Mrs. Jewls.

Joe counted to ten: "six, eight, twelve, one, five, two, seven, eleven, three, ten."

"No, Joe, that is wrong," said Mrs. Jewls.

"No, it isn't," said Joe. "I counted until I got to ten."

"But you were wrong," said Mrs. Jewls. "I'll **prove** it to you." She put five pencils on his desk. "How many pencils do we have here, Joe?"

Joe counted the pencils. "Four, six, one, nine, five. There are five pencils, Mrs. Jewls."

"That's wrong," said Mrs. Jewls.

"How many pencils are there?" Joe asked.

"Five," said Mrs. Jewls.

"That's what I said," said Joe. "May I go to recess now?"

"No," said Mrs. Jewls. "You got the right answer, but you counted the wrong way. You were just lucky." She set eight potatoes on his desk. "How many potatoes, Joe?"

Joe counted the potatoes. "Seven, five, three, one, two, four, six, eight. There are eight potatoes, Mrs. Jewls."

"No, there are eight," said Mrs. Jewls.

"But that's what I said," said Joe. "May I go to recess now?"

"No, you got the right answer, but you counted the wrong way again." She put three books on his desk. "Count the books,

Joe."

Joe counted the books. "A thousand, a million, three. Three, Mrs. Jewls."

"**Correct**," said Mrs. Jewls.

"May I go to recess now?" Joe asked.

"No," said Mrs. Jewls.

"May I have a potato?" asked Joe.

"No. Listen to me. One, two, three, four, five, six, seven, eight, nine, ten," said Mrs. Jewls. "Now you say it."

"One, two, three, four, five, six, seven, eight, nine, ten," said Joe.

"Very good!" said Mrs. Jewls. She put six **eraser**s on his desk. "Now count the erasers, Joe, just the way I showed you."

Joe counted the erasers. "One, two, three, four, five, six, seven, eight, nine, ten. There are ten, Mrs. Jewls."

"No," said Mrs. Jewls.

"Didn't I count right?" asked Joe.

"Yes, you counted right, but you got the wrong answer," said Mrs. Jewls.

"This doesn't **make** any **sense**," said Joe. "When I count the wrong way I get the right answer, and when I count right I get the wrong answer."

Mrs. Jewls hit her head against the wall five times. "How many times did I hit my head against the wall?" she asked.

"One, two, three, four, five, six, seven, eight, nine, ten. You hit your head against the wall ten times," said Joe.

"No," said Mrs. Jewls.

"Four, six, one, nine, five. You hit your head five times," said Joe.

Mrs. Jewls shook her head no and said, "Yes, that is right."

The bell rang, and all the other children came back from recess. The fresh air had made them very excited, and they were laughing and shouting.

"Oh, darn.[1]" said Joe. "Now I missed recess."

"Hey, Joe, where were you?" asked John. "You missed a great game of **kickball**."

"I kicked a home run,[2]" said Todd.

"What was wrong with you, Joe?" asked Joy.

"Nothing," said Joe. "Mrs. Jewls was just trying to teach me how to count."

Joy laughed. "You mean you don't know how to count!"

"Counting is easy," said Maurecia.

"Now, now," said Mrs. Jewls. "What's easy for you may not be easy for Joe, and what's easy for Joe may not be easy for you."

"Nothing's easy for Joe," said Maurecia. "He's stupid."

"I can **beat** you up," said Joe.

"Try it," said Maurecia.

---

1   darn 'damn' 대신에 쓰는 가벼운 욕설로 '젠장할', '빌어먹을'이라는 뜻이다.
2   home run 홈런. 타자의 타구가 파울이 되지 않고 외야 펜스를 넘어가는 경우를 말한다.

"That will be enough of that," said Mrs. Jewls. She wrote Maurecia's name on the **blackboard** under the word **DISCIPLINE**.

Joe put his head on his desk between the eight potatoes and the six erasers.

"Don't feel bad, Joe," said Mrs. Jewls.

"I just don't **get it**," said Joe. "I'll never learn how to count."

"Sure you will, Joe," said Mrs. Jewls. "One day it will just come to you. You'll wake up one morning and suddenly be able to count."

Joe asked, "If all I have to do is wake up, what am I going to school for?"

"School just **speed**s things up," said Mrs. Jewls. "Without school it might take another seventy years before you wake up and are able to count."

"By time I may have no hair left on top of my head to count," said Joe.

"**Exact**ly," said Mrs. Jewls. "That is why you go to school."

When Joe woke up the next day, he knew how to count. He had fifty-five thousand and six hairs on his head. They were all curly.

4. SHARIE

Sharie had long **eyelash**es. She **weigh**ed only forty-nine pounds.[1]
She always wore a big red and blue **overcoat** with a **hood**. The
overcoat weighed thirty-five pounds. The red part weighed fifteen
pounds, the blue part weighed fifteen pounds, and the hood
weighed five pounds. Her eyelashes weighed a pound and a half.

She sat next to the window in Mrs. Jewls's class. She **spent** a
lot of time just **staring** out the window. Mrs. Jewls didn't mind.
Mrs. Jewls said that a lot of people learn best when they stare out

---

1 pound 무게의 단위 파운드. 49파운드는 약 22킬로그램이다.

a window.

Sharie often **fell asleep** in class. Mrs. Jewls didn't mind that, either. She said that a lot of people do their best learning when they are asleep.

Sharie spent all of her time either looking out the window or sleeping. Mrs. Jewls thought she was the best student in the class.

One afternoon it was very hot. All of the windows were open, yet Sharie still wore her red and blue overcoat. The heat made her very tired. Mrs. Jewls was teaching **arithmetic**. Sharie pulled the hood up over her face, **buried** herself in the coat, and went to sleep.

"Mrs. Jewls," said Kathy, "Sharie is asleep."

"That's good," said Mrs. Jewls. "She must be learning something."

Mrs. Jewls continued with the lesson.

Sharie began to **snore**.

"Mrs. Jewls, Sharie is snoring," said Kathy.

"Yes, I can hear her," said Mrs. Jewls. "She must be learning an **awful** lot today. I wish the rest of you could be like her."

Sharie began to **toss and turn**. She **flop**ped over on top of her desk, and then **roll**ed over on top of Kathy's desk. Then she rolled back the other way. Kathy **scream**ed. Sharie rolled out the window. She was still **sound asleep**.

As you know, Mrs. Jewls's class was on the thirtieth story of Wayside School. So Sharie had a long way to go.

After she had fallen ten stories, Sharie woke up. She looked around. She was **confused**. She wasn't in Mrs. Jewls's class, and she wasn't at home in bed. She couldn't **figure out** where she was. She **yawn**ed, pulled the hood back over her eyes, and went back to sleep. By that time she had fallen another ten stories.

Wayside School had an **exceptional**ly large playground. Louis, the **yard** teacher, was **way** over on the other side of it when he happened to see Sharie fall out the window. He **duck**ed under the **volleyball net**, **hurtle**d past the **kickball field**, **hop**ped over the hopscotch[2] **court**, climbed through the monkey bars,[3] **sped** across the grass, and caught Sharie just before she hit the ground.

The people in Mrs. Jewls's class **cheer**ed.

Sharie woke up in Louis's arms.

"Darn it,[4] Louis," she said. "What did you go and wake me up for?"

"I'm sorry, Sharie," said Louis.

"I'm sorry, I'm sorry," Sharie repeated. "Is that all you can say? I was having a wonderful dream until you woke me up. You're always **bother**ing me, Louis. I can't **stand** it." She laughed and hugged him around the neck.

---

2 hopscotch 돌차기 놀이. 바닥에 일정 크기로 바둑판 모양의 칸을 만들고 숫자를 쓴 다음, 순서에 따라 돌을 던져 놓고 한 발로 뛰며 모든 칸을 밟아 돌아오는 게임.

3 monkey bars 정글짐. 아이들이 오르내리며 놀도록 만든 운동 기구. 철봉을 가로세로로 얽어서 만든다.

4 darn it 못마땅하거나 짜증스러울 때 쓰는 비속어 'damn it'을 순화한 표현으로 '에이 참!' 이라고 해석할 수 있다.

Louis carried her back up thirty flights of stairs to Mrs. Jewls's room.

That evening, when Sharie went to bed, she was unable to fall asleep. She just wasn't tired.

5. TODD

All of the children in Mrs. Jewls's class, except Todd, were talking and **carry**ing **on**. Todd was thinking. Todd always thought before he spoke. When he got an idea, his eyes **lit up**.

Todd finished thinking and began to speak. But before he said two words, Mrs. Jewls called him.

"Todd," she said, "you **know better** than to talk in class. You must learn to work quietly, like the other children." She wrote his name on the blackboard under the word DISCIPLINE.

Todd looked around in **amaze**ment. All of the other children, who had been talking and screaming and fighting only seconds earlier, were quietly working in their **workbook**s. Todd **scratch**ed his head.

A child was given three chances in Mrs. Jewls's class. The first time he did something wrong, Mrs. Jewls wrote his name on the blackboard under the word DISCIPLINE. The second time he did something wrong, she put a check next to his name. And the third time he did something wrong, she circled his name.

Todd reached into his desk and pulled out his workbook. He had only just started on it when he felt someone **tap** him on the shoulder. It was Joy.

"What page are you on?" Joy asked.

"Page four," Todd **whisper**ed.

"I'm on page eleven," said Joy.

Todd didn't say anything. He didn't want to get into trouble. He just went back to work.

Five minutes later, Joy tapped him again. Todd **ignore**d her. So Joy **poke**d him in the back with her pencil. Todd **pretend**ed he didn't **notice**. Joy got up from her seat and **sharpen**ed her pencil. She came back and poked it in Todd's back. "What page are you on?" she asked.

"Page five," Todd answered.

"Boy, are you **dumb**," said Joy, "I'm on page twenty-nine."

"It isn't a **race**," Todd whispered.

Five minutes later Joy pulled Todd's hair and didn't let go until he turned around. "What page are you on?" she **demand**ed.

"Page six," Todd answered as quietly as he could.

"I'M ON PAGE TWO HUNDRED!" Joy shouted.

Todd was very angry. "Will you please let me do my work and stop **bother**ing me!"

Mrs. Jewls heard him. "Todd, what did I say about talking in class?"

Todd scratched his head.

Mrs. Jewls put a check next to Todd's name on the blackboard under the word DISCIPLINE.

Todd really tried to be good. He knew that if he talked one more time, Mrs. Jewls would circle his name. Then he'd have to go home early, at twelve o'clock, on the **kindergarten** bus, just as he had the day before and the day before that. In fact, there hadn't been a day since Mrs. Jewls **took over** the class that she didn't send Todd home early. She said she did it for his own good. The other children went home at two o'clock.

Todd wasn't really bad. He just always got caught. He really wanted to stay past twelve o'clock. He wanted to find out what the class did from twelve to two. But it didn't look as though this was going to be his day. It was only ten-thirty, and he already had two **strikes**[1] against him. He **seal**ed his lips and went back to work.

---

1 strike 스트라이크. 야구에서 타자가 타격 기회를 놓치거나 스윙을 하지 못한 공을 말한다. 타자가 스트라이크를 세 번 받으면 아웃된다. 여기서는 세 번의 경고를 받으면 집으로 가는 것을 스트라이크 세 번으로 표현했다.

There was a **knock** on the door. Mrs. Jewls opened it. Two men stepped in wearing masks and holding guns. "Give us all your money!" they demanded.

"All I have is a **nickel**," said Mrs. Jewls.

"I have a **dime**," said Maurecia.

"I have thirteen cents," said Leslie.

"I have four cents," said Dameon.

"What kind of bank is this?" asked one of the **robber**s.

"It's not a bank, it's a school," said Todd. "Can't you read?"

"No," said the robbers.

"Neither can I," said Todd.

"Do you mean we walked **all the way** up thirty flights of stairs for nothing?" asked the robber. "Don't you have anything **valuable**?"

Todd's eyes lit up. "We sure do," he said. "We have **knowledge**." He **grab**bed Joy's workbook and gave it to the robbers. "Knowledge is much more valuable than money."

"Thanks, kid," said one of the robbers.

"Maybe I'll **give up** being a **criminal** and become a scientist," said the other.

They left the room without hurting anybody.

"Now I don't have a workbook," **complain**ed Joy.

Mrs. Jewls gave her a new one. Joy had to start all the way back at the beginning.

"Hey, Joy, what page are you on?" asked Todd.

"Page one," Joy **sigh**ed.

"I'm on page eight," laughed Todd **triumphant**ly.

Mrs. Jewls heard him. She circled his name. Todd had three strikes against him. At twelve o'clock he left the room to go home early on the kindergarten bus.

But this time when he left, he was like a star baseball player leaving the **field**. All the children stood up, **clap**ped their hands, and **whistle**d.

Todd scratched his head.

6. BEBE

Bebe was a girl with short brown hair, a little beebee nose,[1] totally tiny toes, and big brown eyes. Her full name was Bebe Gunn. She was the fastest draw[2] in Mrs. Jewls's class.

She could draw a cat in less than forty-five seconds, a dog in less than thirty, and a flower in less than eight seconds.

But, of course, Bebe never drew just one dog, or one cat, or

---

1 a little beebee nose Bebe Gunn이라는 이름은 BB탄 총(BB gun)과 발음이 같다. 여기서는 이 이름을 활용해 BB탄처럼 조그맣고 동그란 코를 'a little beebee nose'라고 말장난했다.

2 the fastest draw Bebe가 반에서 가장 빨리 그림을 그린다는 의미로 'the fastest draw'라고 표현했다. 이 표현에는 과거 미국 서부시대에 '총을 가장 빨리 뽑는 사람'이라는 의미도 있기 때문에 역시 BB탄 총을 연상시킨다.

one flower. Art was from twelve-thirty to one-thirty. Why, in that time, she could draw fifty cats, a hundred flowers, twenty dogs, and several eggs or watermelons. It took her the same amount of time to draw a watermelon as an egg.

Calvin sat next to Bebe. He didn't think he was very good at art. Why, it took him the whole **period** just to draw one airplane. So instead, he just helped Bebe. He was Bebe's **assistant**. As soon as Bebe would finish one **masterpiece**, Calvin would take it from her and set down a clean **sheet** of paper. Whenever her **crayon** ran low, Calvin was ready with a new crayon. That way Bebe didn't have to **waste** any time. And in return, Bebe would draw five or six airplanes for Calvin.

It was twelve-thirty, time for art. Bebe was ready. On her desk was a sheet of yellow construction paper.[3] In her hand was a green crayon.

Calvin was ready. He held a **stack** of paper and a box of crayons.

"Ready, Bebe," said Calvin.

"Ready, Calvin," said Bebe.

"Okay," said Mrs. Jewls, "time for art."

She had **hardly** finished her sentence when Bebe had already drawn a picture of a **leaf**.

Calvin took it from her and put another piece of paper down.

"Red," called Bebe.

---

3 construction paper 마분지.

Calvin **hand**ed Bebe a red crayon.

"Blue," called Bebe.

He gave her a blue crayon.

They were quite a pair. Their teamwork was **remarkable**. Bebe drew pictures as fast as Calvin could pick up the old paper and set down the new—a fish, an apple, three cherries, bing,[4] bing, bing.

At one-thirty Mrs. Jewls **announced**, "Okay, class, art is over."

Bebe dropped her crayon and fell over on her desk. Calvin **sigh**ed and **lean**ed back in his chair. He could hardly move. They had **broken** their old **record**. Bebe had drawn three hundred and seventy-eight pictures. They lay in a **pile** on Calvin's desk.

Mrs. Jewls walked by. "Calvin, did you draw all these pictures?"

Calvin laughed. "No, I can't draw. Bebe drew them all."

"Well, then, what did you draw?" asked Mrs. Jewls.

"I didn't draw anything," said Calvin.

"Why not? Don't you like art?" asked Mrs. Jewls.

"I love art," said Calvin. "That's why I didn't draw anything."

Mrs. Jewls did not understand.

"It would have taken me the whole period just to draw one picture," said Calvin. "And Bebe would only have been able to draw a hundred pictures. But with the two of us working together, she was able to draw three hundred and seventy-eight pictures!

---

4 bing 빙 체리. 주로 미국에서 재배되는 체리의 한 종류.

That's a lot more art."

Bebe and Calvin **shook hands**.

"No," said Mrs. Jewls. "That isn't how you **measure** art. It isn't how many pictures you have, but how good the pictures are. Why, a person could **spend** his whole life just drawing one picture of a cat. In that time I'm sure Bebe could draw a million cats."

"Two million," said Bebe.

Mrs. Jewls continued. "But if that one picture is better than each of Bebe's two million, then that person has produced more art than Bebe."

Bebe looked as if she was going to cry. She picked up all the pictures from Calvin's desk and threw them in the **garbage**. Then she ran from the room.

"I thought her pictures were good," said Calvin. He reached into the garbage **pail** and took out a **crumple**d-up picture of an airplane.

Bebe walked outside into the **playground**.

Louis, the yard teacher, **spot**ted her. "Where are you going?" he asked.

"I'm going home to draw a picture of a cat," said Bebe.

"Will you bring it to school and show it to me tomorrow?" Louis asked.

"Tomorrow!" laughed Bebe. "By tomorrow I **doubt** if I'll even be finished with one **whisker**."

7. CALVIN

Calvin had a big, round face.

"Calvin," said Mrs. Jewls, "I want you to take this note to Miss Zarves for me."

"Miss Zarves?" asked Calvin.

"Yes, Miss Zarves," said Mrs. Jewls. "You know where she is, don't you?"

"Yes," said Calvin. "She's on the nineteenth **story**."

"That's right, Calvin," said Mrs. Jewls. "Take it to her."

Calvin didn't move.

"Well, what are you waiting for?" asked Mrs. Jewls.

"She's on the nineteenth story," said Calvin.

"Yes, we have already **establish**ed that fact," said Mrs. Jewls.

"The nineteenth story," Calvin repeated.

"Yes, Calvin, the nineteenth story," said Mrs. Jewls. "Now take it to her before I lose my **patience**."

"But, Mrs. Jewls," said Calvin.

"Now, Calvin!" said Mrs. Jewls. "Unless you would rather go home on the **kindergarten** bus."

"Yes, ma'am," said Calvin. Slowly he walked out the door.

"Ha, ha, ha," laughed Terrence, "take it to the nineteenth story."

"Give it to Miss Zarves," **hoot**ed Myron.

"Have fun on the nineteenth story," called Jason.

Calvin stood outside the door to the classroom. He didn't know where to go.

As you know, when the **builder** built Wayside School, he **accidental**ly built it **sideways**. But he also forgot to build the nineteenth story. He built the eighteenth and the twentieth, but no nineteenth. He said he was very sorry.

There was also no Miss Zarves. Miss Zarves taught the class on the nineteenth story. Since there was no nineteenth story, there was no Miss Zarves.

And **besides** that, as if Calvin didn't have enough problems, there was no note. Mrs. Jewls had never given Calvin the note.

"Boy, this is just great," thought Calvin. "Just great! I'm supposed to take a note that I don't have to a teacher who doesn't exist, and who teaches on a story that was never built."

He didn't know what to do. He walked down to the eighteenth story, then back up to the twentieth, then back down to the eighteenth, and back up again to the twentieth. There was no nineteenth story. There never was a nineteenth story. And there never will be a nineteenth story.

Calvin walked down to the **administration** office. He decided to put the note in Miss Zarves's **mailbox**. But there wasn't one of those, either. That didn't bother Calvin too much, however, since he didn't have a note.

He looked out the window and saw Louis, the yard teacher, **shoot**ing **baskets**. "Louis will know what to do," he thought. Calvin went outside.

"Hey, Louis," Calvin called.

"Hi, Calvin," said Louis. He **toss**ed him the basketball. Calvin **dribble**d up and **took a shot**. He missed. Louis **tip**ped it in.

"Do you want to play a game?" Louis asked.

"I don't have time," said Calvin. "I have to **deliver** a note to Miss Zarves up on the nineteenth story."

"Then what are you doing all the way down here?" Louis asked.

"There is no nineteenth story," said Calvin.

"Then where is Miss Zarves?" asked Louis.

"There is no Miss Zarves," said Calvin.

"What are you going to do with the note?" asked Louis.

"There is no note," said Calvin.

"I understand," said Louis.

"That's good," said Calvin, "because I sure don't."

"It's very simple," said Louis. "You are not supposed to take no notes to no teachers. You already haven't done it."

Calvin still didn't understand. "I'll just have to tell Mrs. Jewls that I couldn't deliver the note," he said.

"That's good," said Louis. "The truth is always best. Besides, I don't think I understand what I said, either."

Calvin walked back up the thirty **flights of stairs** to Mrs. Jewls's class.

"Thank you very much, Calvin," said Mrs. Jewls.

Calvin said, "But I—"

Mrs. Jewls **interrupt**ed him. "That was a very important note, and I'm glad I was able to **count on** you."

"Yes, but you see—" said Calvin.

"You delivered the note to Miss Zarves on the nineteenth story?" asked Jason. "How did you do it?"

"What do you mean, how did he do it?" asked Mrs. Jewls. "He gave Miss Zarves the note. Some people, Jason, are **responsible**."

"But you see, Mrs. Jewls—" said Calvin.

"The note was very important," said Mrs. Jewls. "I told Miss Zarves not to meet me for lunch."

"Don't worry," said Calvin. "She won't."

"Good," said Mrs. Jewls. "I have a coffee can full of Tootsie

Roll pops[1] on my desk. You may **help yourself** to one, for being such a good **messenger**."

"Thanks," said Calvin, "but really, it was nothing."

---

1 Tootsie Roll pop 툿시 롤 팝. 초콜릿 캔디의 이름.

8. MYRON

Myron had big ears. He was **elect**ed class **president**. The children in Mrs. Jewls's class **expect**ed him to be a good president. Other presidents were good speakers. Myron was even better. He was a good listener.

But he had a problem. He didn't know what a class president was supposed to do. So he asked.

"What am I supposed to do?"

"It's a difficult job," said Mrs. Jewls. "But you can do it. You must turn the lights on every morning and turn them off at the end of the day."

"What?" asked Myron.

"As a class president you must learn to listen," said Mrs. Jewls. "I'll repeat myself only one more time. You must turn the lights on every morning—"

"I heard you the first time," said Myron. "It just doesn't sound like much of a job."

"It **certain**ly is!" said Mrs. Jewls. "Without light I can't teach, and the children can't learn. Only you can give us that light. I think it is a very important job."

"I guess so," said Myron. He wasn't **convince**d.

"Here, let me show you how to work a light switch," said Mrs. Jewls.

"I already know how," said Myron. "I've been turning lights on and off all my life."

"Very good!" said Mrs. Jewls. "You'll make a fine president."

Myron wanted to be the best president ever. But it was such an easy job, he thought, that anybody could do it. When school **let out** that day, Myron stayed behind. He **turn**ed **out** the lights by **flick**ing the switch down.

"Excellent!" said Mrs. Jewls.

On his way home, Myron heard a **horrible** noise. First there was a loud **screech**ing, then a sharp **squeal**, a **roar**ing engine, and then the very **faint** sound of a girl crying.

Myron ran to see what had happened.

Dana was **bent** over in the middle of the road.

"What's the **matter**?" asked Myron.

"My dog, Pugsy, was hit by a car," Dana cried.

"Who did it?" asked Myron.

"I don't know!" Dana **sob**bed. "They **sped** away."

"Well, that's not important," said Myron. "We've got to try to save Pugsy."

Pugsy lay **unconscious** in the street. Myron **careful**ly picked her up. He carried her two miles[1] to the **vet**. Dana cried at his side.

"Don't worry, Dana," said Myron. "She'll be all right." But he wasn't really so sure.

He gave Pugsy to the vet, walked Dana home, then walked home himself.

Dana was so upset that she forgot to thank him. Myron didn't mind. He thought that was what being class president was all about.

The next morning, before he went to school, Myron went to Dana's house. Pugsy was there. She seemed all right.

Dana **pet**ted her. Pugsy **lick**ed her face.

"See, Myron, she's all right," said Dana. "The vet said that you brought her in just **in time**."

"Hi, Pugsy," said Myron. He petted her.

Pugsy **bit** his hand.

"I guess she doesn't know you," said Dana. "She was unconscious

---

1 mile 거리의 단위 마일. 2마일은 약 3.2킬로미터이다.

yesterday when you saved her life."

Dana's mother put some **medicine** and a Band-Aid[2] on Myron's hand. Then she drove the children to school.

They were late. They ran up the stairs to Mrs. Jewls's class. The room was **completely** dark.

"It's about time you got here, Myron," said Mrs. Jewls. "We have no lights."

"Why didn't somebody else just turn them on?" asked Myron.

"Because you're class president," said Mrs. Jewls. "Show Stephen how to work the lights. From now on he will be class president."

Myron showed Stephen how to turn on the lights. He flicked the switch up.

At the end of the day, Myron showed Stephen how to turn the lights off. He flicked the switch down.

After a week, Stephen finally **caught on**. He made a good president. The lights were on every morning.

Myron, who was president for only a day, was the best president in the history of Wayside School. It was just that nobody knew it.

---

2 Band-Aid 밴드에이드. 원래는 반창고의 상표명이었으나, 반창고를 뜻하는 일반명사처럼 쓰인다.

9. MAURECIA

Maurecia liked ice cream. She was sweet and pretty and could **beat** up any boy in Mrs. Jewls's class. Everybody liked Maurecia— except Kathy, but then she didn't like anybody. Maurecia only liked ice cream.

Every day Maurecia brought an ice cream cone to school and kept it in her desk until lunch time. At first she brought chocolate ice cream every day. But she soon tired of chocolate ice cream. So she started bringing vanilla. But she got tired of vanilla, too. Then she got tired of strawberry, fudge **ripple**,[1] butter pecan,[2] pistachio,[3] and burgundy cherry,[4] in that order.

And then a **terrible** thing happened. Maurecia got tired of ice cream. By that time her desk was a **mess**, and everything in it was **sticky**.

Everybody liked Maurecia. But Maurecia didn't like anything. Mrs. Jewls hated to see Maurecia unhappy.

"I don't understand it, Mrs. Jewls," cried Maurecia. "There just aren't any good **flavor**s anymore."

So Mrs. Jewls worked all night. The next day she brought in a new flavor of ice cream for Maurecia. It was Maurecia-flavored ice cream. "Everybody will like it," thought Mrs. Jewls, "because everybody likes Maurecia."

"Here you are, Maurecia," said Mrs. Jewls, "Maurecia-flavored ice cream."

Everybody gathered around as Maurecia tasted it. They hoped she'd like it.

Maurecia took a **lick**.

"Well?" said Mrs. Jewls.

Maurecia took another lick.

"Well?" asked the class.

"This ice cream has no taste," said Maurecia. "It doesn't taste bad, but it doesn't taste good. It doesn't taste like anything at all!"

---

1   fudge ripple 설탕과 초콜릿으로 만든 캔디인 퍼지가 물결(ripple)처럼 들어간 아이스크림.
2   butter pecan 버터와 호두(pecan)가 들어간 아이스크림.
3   pistachio 피스타치오. 견과류로 그린아몬드라고도 하며, 아몬드와 비슷한 풍미를 가지고 있다. 열매는 녹색으로 타원형이고 과자와 아이스크림 등을 만드는데 사용한다.
4   burgundy cherry 체리, 와인, 꿀 등을 섞은 소스가 들어간 아이스크림.

Mrs. Jewls was **heartbroken**.

"Here, let me try it," said Todd. He tasted it. "You're crazy, Maurecia!" he said. "This is the best-tasting ice cream I've ever eaten! Try some, Deedee."

"Ummmmmmmmm, it's delicious," said Deedee. "It's so sweet and **creamy**." She passed it around the room.

"Oh, it is so good," said Leslie.

"I think it tastes terrible," said Kathy.

"I don't understand it," said Maurecia. "I don't taste a thing."

Mrs. Jewls **slap**ped herself in the face. "Oh, I've made a big mistake, Maurecia. Of course you can't taste anything. It's Maurecia-flavored ice cream. It's the same taste you always taste when you're not tasting anything at all."

So the next day Mrs. Jewls brought in Joe-flavored ice cream. Maurecia liked it. So did everybody else. Joe thought it had no taste.

Everybody liked Maurecia. Maurecia only liked Joe.

The following day Mrs. Jewls brought in Ron-flavored ice cream. Ron thought it had no taste, but everybody else loved it.

Everybody liked Maurecia. Maurecia only liked Joe and Ron.

By the end of the month, Mrs. Jewls had brought in twenty-seven new flavors of ice cream, one for each member of the class.

Everybody liked Maurecia, and Maurecia liked everybody. They all tasted so good. All except Kathy, that is. Kathy-flavored ice cream tasted a little bit like old bologna.[5]

Everyone still agreed that Maurecia-flavored ice cream was the best, except Maurecia. She liked Todd ice cream the best.

This **turned out** to be a problem. **Every once in a while** Maurecia would try to take a **bite** out of Todd's arm in order to get that very special flavor.

---

5   bologna 볼로냐 소시지. 이탈리아의 도시 볼로냐(Bologna)에서 유래했다.

10. PAUL

Paul had the best seat in Mrs. Jewls's class. He sat in the back of the room. It was the seat that was the farthest away from Mrs. Jewls.

Mrs. Jewls was teaching the class about **fraction**s. She drew a picture of a pie on the **blackboard**. She cut the pie into eight pieces. She explained that each piece was one-eighth of the pie.

Paul never **paid attention**. He didn't see the picture of the pie. He didn't see anything.

Well, he did see one thing.

Actually, he saw two things.

He saw Leslie's two **pigtail**s.

Leslie sat in front of Paul. She had two long, brown pigtails that reached **all the way** down to her **waist**.

Paul saw those pigtails, and a terrible **urge came over** him. He wanted to pull a pigtail. He wanted to **wrap** his **fist** around it, feel the hair between his fingers, and just **yank**.

He thought it would also be fun to **tie** the pigtails together, or better yet, tie them to her chair. But most of all, he just wanted to pull one.

Slowly he reached for the one on the right. "NO! What am I doing?" he thought. "I'll only get into trouble."

Paul had it made. He sat in the back of the room. He paid no attention to anyone, and nobody paid any attention to him. But if he pulled a pigtail, it would be all over. Leslie would **tell on** him, and he'd become the center of attention.

He **sigh**ed and slowly **withdrew** his arm.

But Paul couldn't **ignore** those pigtails. There they were, **dangling** right in front of him, just **beg**ging to be pulled. He could close his eyes, but he couldn't make the pigtails disappear. He could still smell them. And hear them. He could almost taste them.

"Maybe just a little **tug**," he thought. "No, none."

There they hung, easily within his reach.

"Well let them just hang there!" thought Paul.

It would be **foolish** to pull one, no **matter** how **tempting** they were. None of the other children in the class pulled pigtails; why should he? Of course, none of the other children sat behind Leslie, either.

It was just a simple matter of being able to think clearly. That was all. Paul **thought** it **over** and decided not to pull one. It was as simple as that.

Suddenly his arm **shot** forward. He **grab**bed Leslie's right pigtail and yanked.

"Yaaaaaahhhhhhhhhh!" **scream**ed Leslie.

Everybody looked at her.

"Paul pulled my pigtail," she said.

They all looked at Paul.

"I . . . I couldn't help it," said Paul.

"You'd better learn to help it," said Mrs. Jewls. She wrote Paul's name on the blackboard under the word **DISCIPLINE**. "Tell Leslie you're sorry."

"I'm sorry, Leslie," said Paul.

"Hmmmph," said Leslie.

Paul felt horrible. Never again would he pull another pigtail! Except, there was one problem. He still wasn't **satisfied**. He had pulled the right one, but that wasn't enough. He wanted to pull the left one, too. It was as if he heard a little voice coming from the pigtail saying, "Pull me, Paul. Pull me."

"I can't," Paul answered. "My name's already on the blackboard under the word DISCIPLINE."

"**Big deal**," said the pigtail. "Pull me."

46

"**No way**," said Paul. "Never again."

"Aw, **come on**, Paul, just a little tug," urged the pigtail. "What **harm** could it do?"

"Lots of harm," said Paul. "Leslie will scream, and I'll get in trouble again."

"Boy, that's not fair," **whine**d the pigtail. "You pulled the right one. Now it's my turn."

"I know, but I can't," said Paul.

"Sure you can," said the pigtail. "Just grab me and yank."

"No," said Paul. "It's not right."

"Sure it is, Paul," said the pigtail. "Pigtails are meant to be pulled. That's what we're here for."

"Tell that to Leslie," said Paul.

"Leslie won't mind," said the pigtail. "I promise."

"**I bet**," said Paul. "Just like she didn't mind the last time."

"You just didn't pull hard enough," said the pigtail. "Leslie likes us pulled real hard."

"Really?" asked Paul.

"**Cross my heart**," said the pigtail, "the harder, the better."

"Okay," said Paul. "but if you're lying . . ."

"I promise," said the pigtail.

Paul grabbed the left pigtail. It felt good in his hand. He pulled as hard as he could.

"Yaaaaaaaaaahhhhhhhhhhhhhhhhhhhhhh!!!" screamed Leslie.

Mrs. Jewls asked, "Paul, did you pull Leslie's pigtail again?"

"No," said Paul. "I pulled the other one."

All the children laughed.

"Are you trying to be funny?" asked Mrs. Jewls.

"No," said Paul. "I was trying to be fair. I couldn't pull one and not the other."

The children laughed again.

"Pigtails are meant to be pulled," Paul **conclud**ed.

Mrs. Jewls put a check next to Paul's name on the blackboard under the word DISCIPLINE.

But at last Paul was satisfied. True, his name was on the blackboard with a check next to it, but that really didn't matter. All he had to do was stay out of trouble the rest of the day, and his name would be **erase**d. It's easy to stay out of trouble when you have the best seat in the class.

In fact, Paul could do this every day. He could pull Leslie's pigtails twice, and then stay out of trouble the rest of the day. There was nothing Leslie could do about it.

Suddenly, **out of nowhere**, Leslie screamed, "Yaaaahhhhhhhh!"

Mrs. Jewls circled Paul's name and sent him home early on the kindergarten bus. Nobody would believe that he hadn't pulled Leslie's pigtail again.

11. DANA

Dana had four beautiful eyes. She wore glasses. But her eyes were so beautiful that the glasses only made her prettier. With two eyes she was pretty. With four eyes she was beautiful. With six eyes she would have been even more beautiful. And if she had a hundred eyes, all over her face and her arms and her feet, why, she would have been the most beautiful **creature** in the world.

But poor Dana wasn't **cover**ed from head to foot with beautiful eyes. She was covered with **mosquito bite**s.

Mrs. Jewls picked up her **yardstick** and said, "Now it's time for **arithmetic**."

"Oh, no, Mrs. Jewls," said Dana. "I can't do arithmetic. I **itch** all over. I can't **concentrate**."

"But we have all kinds of arithmetic," said Mrs. Jewls, "addition without **carry**ing, addition with carrying, and carrying without addition."

"I don't care," cried Dana.

"We have that, too," said Mrs. Jewls, "addition without caring. Now, stop **carrying on**."

Dana **whine**d, "I can't, Mrs. Jewls. I itch too much."

"And I'm too **thirsty**," said D.J.

"I'm too tired," said Ron.

"I'm too hungry," said Terrence.

"I'm too stupid," said Todd.

Mrs. Jewls hit her desk with her yardstick. Everyone stopped talking.

Mrs. Jewls said, "We are going to have arithmetic now, and I don't want to hear another thing about it."

"But, Mrs. Jewls, I really do itch. I can't do arithmetic," Dana whined.

"No," said Mrs. Jewls. "Arithmetic is the best known **cure** for an itch. How many mosquito bites do you have?"

"I don't know," said Dana, "over a hundred. First I try **scratch**ing one, but then another one starts to itch. So I scratch that one, and that one stops, and another one starts. So I scratch that one, and the itch moves down to another one. Then it goes back to the first one. The itch just never stays in the same place. I just can't scratch them all."

"What you need is a good, strong **dose** of arithmetic," said Mrs. Jewls.

"I'd rather have calamine lotion,[1]" said Dana.

"Remember, Dana," said Mrs. Jewls, "mosquito bites itch, not numbers."

"So what?" said Dana.

Mrs. Jewls continued. "We'll just have to **turn** your mosquito bites **into** numbers."

"I'm a **mess**," Dana **moan**ed.

Mrs. Jewls began to turn the mosquito bites into numbers. "How much is three mosquito bites plus three mosquito bites?" she asked.

Rondi raised her hand. "Six mosquito bites," she answered.

"How much is six mosquito bites minus two mosquito bites?" asked Mrs. Jewls.

"Four mosquito bites," said D.J.

"How much is five mosquito bites times two?" asked Mrs. Jewls.

"Ten mosquito bites," said Bebe.

"Very good," said Mrs. Jewls.

"I still itch," Dana **complain**ed.

---

1 calamine lotion 칼라민 로션. 햇볕에 탔거나 따가운 피부에 바르는 분홍색 약물.

"I've got one more question," said Mrs. Jewls. "How much is forty-nine mosquito bites plus seventy-five mosquito bites?"

Nobody raised a hand.

"Think, class," said Mrs. Jewls. "This is for Dana."

Nobody knew the answer. Dana's itch began to get worse and worse.

At last, Dana began **count**ing her own mosquito bites. She counted seventy-five on one side and forty-nine on the other. Then she added them together for a total of one hundred and twenty-four mosquito bites.

"One hundred and twenty-four mosquito bites," Dana called.

"Very good," said Mrs. Jewls.

Dana had one hundred and twenty-four mosquito bites. And none of them itched anymore.

"I'm still thirsty," said D.J. "Can arithmetic do anything for that?"

"I'm still tired," said Ron.

"I'm still hungry," said Terrence.

"I'm still stupid," said Todd.

"I'm glad we turned my mosquito bites into numbers instead of letters," said Dana. "I could never **spell** *mosquito.*"

12. JASON

Jason had a small face and a big mouth. He had the second biggest mouth in Mrs. Jewls's class. And there were an **awful** lot of big mouths in that class.

"Mrs. Jewls," Jason called without raising his hand. "Joy is **chew**ing gum in class!"

Joy had the biggest mouth in Mrs. Jewls's class. And it was filled with gum. There was **hardly** even **room** for her **tongue**.

"Joy, I'm **ashamed** of you," said Mrs. Jewls. "I'm afraid I'll have to put your name up on the board."

"That's okay, Mrs. Jewls," Jason called. "I'll do it." Jason **hop**ped out of his seat and wrote Joy's name on the blackboard under the word DISCIPLINE.

While he was up, Joy took the **glob** of gum out of her mouth and placed it on Jason's chair.

Rondi and Allison **giggle**d.

Jason walked back from the blackboard to his desk and sat down. "Mrs. Jewls," he called, "I'm STUCK!"

Rondi and Allison giggled again.

Mrs. Jewls got angry. "Joy, you're going home on the **kindergarten** bus today."

"Oh, good," said Todd. "I'll have some **company**." Todd went home on the kindergarten bus every day. He could never seem to make it to twelve o'clock without getting into trouble three times. His name wasn't even up on the blackboard yet. But he knew that by twelve o'clock it would be up, checked, and circled.

"Mrs. Jewls, what am I going to do? I'm stuck! I'm going to have to stay here the rest of my life!" said Jason.

"Joy, tell Jason you're sorry," said Mrs. Jewls.

"I'm sorry, Jason," said Joy.

"Oh, that's okay, Joy," said Jason. "I don't mind."

"Try to get up, Jason," said Mrs. Jewls.

Jason tried. "I can't, Mrs. Jewls. I'm stuck."

Mrs. Jewls asked the three Erics to help. Eric Fry and Eric Ovens pulled Jason. Eric Bacon held the chair.

"Stop," cried Jason. "You'll **rip** my pants."

54

Rondi and Allison giggled.

"All right," said Mrs. Jewls. "Let's try ice water. That should **freeze** the gum and make it less **sticky**. I'll go get some from Miss Mush."

Miss Mush was the lunch teacher at Wayside School. She had the **remarkable** ability to **undercook** a **dish** and **overcook** it at the same time. Her **specialty** was a nice, hot **bowl** of mud. She called it porridge.[1]

Jason looked at Rondi and Allison. "No, Mrs. Jewls," he said. "Don't leave me. **Besides**, Miss Mush's ice water is probably warm."

"Don't be **silly**, Jason," said Mrs. Jewls. "I'm sure it will be at least as cold as her soups."

Rondi and Allison **leer**ed at Jason.

"No, Mrs. Jewls, don't go!" **begg**ed Jason.

"I'll be right back, Jason," said Mrs. Jewls. She went to Miss Mush for some ice water.

As soon as Mrs. Jewls stepped out the door, Rondi and Allison jumped up from their seats and started to **tickle** Jason. He laughed until his hair turned purple. The girls got back to their seats just as Mrs. Jewls returned.

Mrs. Jewls carried a big **bucket** of ice cold water.

"Oh, no, please don't, no!" Jason **plead**ed.

---

1 **porridge** 포리지. 귀리에 우유나 물을 부어 걸쭉하게 죽처럼 끓인 음식으로 주로 아침식사로 먹는다.

"We have no choice," said Mrs. Jewls. She threw the water all over him.

"Well," said Mrs. Jewls, "try to get up."

Jason was **drench**ed. "I'm wet and I'm cold and I'm still stuck!"

"Oh, well, it didn't work," said Mrs. Jewls. "At least we tried. Now I guess we'll have to cut your pants off."

Rondi and Allison giggled.

"No, Mrs. Jewls, no!" Jason screamed. "I don't mind being stuck here. I'm really very comfortable."

"Don't be silly, Jason," said Mrs. Jewls.

"Don't cut off my pants," said Jason.

"The three Erics can carry you to the bathroom," said Mrs. Jewls. "I'll ask Louis to call your mother. She can bring you a new pair of pants."

The three Erics took hold of Jason's chair and turned him **upside down**.

"No, Mrs. Jewls," said Jason. "Now I'll always have a place to sit down. I won't have to worry about finding a seat on the bus."

The three Erics began to take him away.

"Wait," said Joy. "Mrs. Jewls, if I can get Jason unstuck, do I still have to go home on the kindergarten bus?"

"All right," said Mrs. Jewls. "If you can somehow get Jason free, you don't have to go home early."

"Don't trust her, Mrs. Jewls," said Jason. He was still hanging upside down.

"I'll just kiss him," said Joy.

"No!" Jason screamed. "Don't let her kiss me, Mrs. Jewls. Throw water on me. Tickle me. Cut off my pants. Hang me upside down from the **ceiling**. But don't let her kiss me!"

"I'll just kiss him on the nose," said Joy.

"We've got nothing to lose, Jason," said Mrs. Jewls.

"Oooooh, who would want to kiss Jason!" said Allison.

Jason hung **helpless**ly upside down.

Joy stepped up and kissed him on the nose.

Jason fell out of the chair and hit his head on the floor.

Rondi and Allison giggled.

"Darn," said Todd. "Now I'll have to go home alone again."

Joy **erase**d her name from the blackboard.

13. RONDI

Rondi had twenty-two beautiful teeth. Everyone else had twenty-four. Rondi was missing her two front teeth. And those were the most beautiful teeth of all.

"Your front teeth are so cute," said Mrs. Jewls. "They make you look just **adorable**."

"But, Mrs. Jewls," said Rondi. "I don't have any front teeth."

"I know," said Mrs. Jewls. "That's what makes them so cute."

Rondi didn't understand.

"Oooh, Rondi, I just love your two front teeth," said Maurecia. "I wish I had some like that."

"But I don't have them," said Rondi.

"That's why I love them so much," said Maurecia.

"Oh, this is silly," said Rondi. "Everybody thinks the teeth I don't have are cute. I'm not wearing a coat. Don't you all just love my coat? And what about my third arm? I don't have one. Isn't it lovely?"

"Love your hat, Rondi," said Joy.

"I'm not wearing a hat!" Rondi screamed.

"That's what makes it so interesting," said Joy. "Don't you think so, Leslie?"

"Oh, yes," said Leslie. "It's a very nice hat. Nice boots, too."

"I'm not wearing boots!" Rondi **insist**ed.

"Yes," said Joy, "very nice boots. They go so well with your hat."

"What hat?" asked Rondi.

"Yes," Leslie agreed. "Rondi showed excellent taste by not wearing the hat or the boots. They go so well together."

Rondi **had had enough**. She covered her head so nobody could see her hat. She put her feet under her desk so nobody could see her boots. Then she closed her mouth tightly so nobody could see her two front teeth.

Suddenly, everybody who was sitting near her began to laugh.

"What's so funny?" asked Todd.

"The joke Rondi didn't tell," said Jason.

"Ask Rondi not to tell it again, Todd," said Calvin.

"Rondi," said Todd, "don't tell it again."

Rondi was **horrified**. She didn't know what to do. She kept her mouth shut and just **stare**d at Todd. To her **amaze**ment, Todd laughed.

"Hey, everybody," called Todd. "Listen to Rondi's joke."

Rondi didn't say a word, but the rest of the class began to laugh.

Mrs. Jewls got very angry. She wrote Rondi's name on the blackboard under the word DISCIPLINE.

"The classroom is not the place for jokes," she said.

"But, Mrs. Jewls," said Rondi. "I didn't tell a joke."

"Yes, I know," said Mrs. Jewls, "but the funniest jokes are the ones that **remain untold**."

"Okay, okay," said Rondi. "If that's what you want, then that's what you'll get. I'll really tell a joke. That way I won't **disturb** the class. And tomorrow I'll wear boots and a hat. Of course, you won't like them as much as the ones I didn't wear today. But I better hurry up and tell my joke before you all start to laugh.

"There was a monkey sitting in a banana tree. He was very hungry. He knew that somewhere in the tree there was a magic banana, and that once he ate that banana, he wouldn't be hungry anymore. He ate one banana. That wasn't it. He was still hungry. He ate another banana. That one wasn't it, either. He was still hungry. Finally, after he ate his tenth banana, he wasn't hungry anymore. 'I knew I'd find it,' he said. 'It's too bad I didn't eat that one first. I wouldn't have had to **waste** all those other bananas.'"

Nobody laughed. Nobody had even listened to Rondi. Mrs. Jewls was busy teaching arithmetic, and everybody else was **pay**ing **strict attention**.

Rondi **slap**ped herself in the face to make sure she was really there. She was.

The bell rang for **recess**. Rondi ran outside. She was very upset.

Louis, the **yard** teacher, saw her. "Why the **frown**, Rondi?" he asked. "**Come on**, smile. Let me see your cute front teeth."

Rondi screamed. She **sock**ed Louis in the **stomach**, then **bit** his arm with her missing teeth. And that kind of bite hurts the worst.

14. SAMMY

It was a **horrible, stinky,** rainy day. Some rainy days are fun and exciting, but not this one. This one **stunk.** All the children were wet and wore **smelly raincoat**s. The whole room smelled **awful.**

"Ooooh, it stinks in here," said Maurecia.

Everybody laughed. But she was right.

There was one good thing, however. There was a new boy in class. New kids are always fun. Except no one could even tell what the new boy looked like. He was **complete**ly covered by his raincoat.

"Class," said Mrs. Jewls. "I'd like you all to meet Sammy.

Let us show him what a nice class we can be."

Leslie walked up and smiled at Sammy. But her smile quickly turned into a **frown**. "You smell **terrible**," she said.

"Leslie!" **exclaim**ed Mrs. Jewls. "That's no way to **greet** a new member of our class." Mrs. Jewls wrote Leslie's name on the **blackboard** under the word **DISCIPLINE**.

"But he does, Mrs. Jewls," said Leslie. "He smells awful."

"You're ugly," Sammy **replied**.

"Now, Sammy, that's no way to talk," said Mrs. Jewls. "Leslie's a very pretty girl."

"She's ugly," said Sammy.

Allison spoke up. "Well, you smell terrible and are probably even uglier. But nobody can see you because you are hiding under that smelly old raincoat."

"That will be enough of that," said Mrs. Jewls. "Now, Sammy, why don't you take off your coat and hang it in the **closet**? Let us all see how nice you look."

"I don't want to, you old **windbag**," said Sammy.

"That's because he's so ugly," said Leslie.

"I'm sure he's quite handsome," said Mrs. Jewls. "He's just **shy**. Here, let me help you." Mrs. Jewls took off Sammy's coat for him. But **underneath** it was still another raincoat, even dirtier and smellier than the first one.

They still couldn't see his face.

"Ooooh, now he smells even worse," said Maurecia.

"You don't **exact**ly smell like a rose, either," Sammy replied.

Mrs. Jewls took off his second raincoat, but there was still another one under that. And the smell became so bad that Mrs. Jewls had to run and **stick** her head **out** the window to get some fresh air.

"You're all a **bunch** of pigs!" Sammy **screech**ed. "Dirty, **rotten** pigs!"

The smell was **overpower**ing. Sammy just stood there, hidden under his raincoats.

Mrs. Jewls wrote Sammy's name under the word DISCIPLINE.

"Send him home on the kindergarten bus," said Joy.

"Not with me," said Todd.

Mrs. Jewls held her nose, walked up to Sammy, and **removed** his raincoat. She threw it out the window. But he had on still another one.

Sammy **hiss**ed. "Hey, old windbag, watch where you throw my good clothes!"

Mrs. Jewls put a check next to Sammy's name on the blackboard. Then she took off another raincoat and threw it out the window. The smell got worse, for he had on still another one.

Sammy began to laugh. His horrible laugh was even worse than his horrible voice.

When Sammy first came into the room, he was four feet[1]

---

1 feet 길이의 단위 피트. 4피트는 121.92센티미터이다.

tall. But after Mrs. Jewls removed six of his raincoats, he was only three feet tall. And there were still more raincoats to go.

Mrs. Jewls circled his name and removed another coat. She threw it out the window. Then she put a triangle around the circle and threw another one of his coats outside. She kept doing this until Sammy was only one-and-a-half feet high. With every coat she took off, Sammy's laugh got louder and the smell got worse.

Some of the children held their ears. Others could hold only one ear because they were holding their nose with the other hand. It was hard to say which was worse, the laugh or the smell.

Sammy stopped laughing and said, "Hey, old windbag, if you take off one more of my coats and throw it out the window, I'll bite your head off."

"They smell too bad for me to allow them in my classroom," said Mrs. Jewls. "You can pick them up when you leave."

"They smell better than you do, Pighead!²" Sammy shouted.

Mrs. Jewls didn't stop. She took off another one of his coats, then another, and another. Sammy was only four inches³ tall, three inches tall, two inches tall. At last she removed the final coat.

All that was there was a dead rat.

"Well, I don't allow dead rats in my classroom," said Mrs.

---

2   pighead 완고한 사람 또는 고집이 센 사람.
3   inch 길이의 단위 인치. 4인치는 10.16센티미터이다.

Jewls. She picked it up by the tail, put it in a plastic bag,[4] and threw it away.

Mrs. Jewls didn't allow dead rats in her class. Todd once brought in a dead rat for show-and-tell,[5] and Mrs. Jewls made him throw that one away, too.

"I'm glad Sammy isn't allowed in our classroom," said Rondi. "I didn't like him very much."

"Yes," said Mrs. Jewls, "we caught another one."

Dead rats were always trying to **sneak** into Mrs. Jewls's class. That was the third one she'd caught since September.

---

4   plastic bag 비닐봉지.
5   show-and-tell 학교 수업 활동의 하나로 학생들이 각자 물건을 가져 와서 발표하는 것을 말한다.

15. DEEDEE

This story **contains** a problem and a **solution**.

Deedee was a **mousey** looking kid. Unlike most children at Wayside School, she liked recess better than **spell**ing. As soon as the recess bell rang, she would jump up from her seat and run out the door.

There were big **sign**s in Wayside School on every floor, "NO JUMPING DOWN THE STAIRS."

Deedee never seemed to **notice** the signs. She jumped down the stairs. Some children took the stairs two at a time. Deedee took them ten at a time. That was on the way down. It was funny. She never seemed to be in quite the same hurry on the way back up.

There was another sign at Wayside School. "NO **CUTTING ACROSS** THE GRASS." Deedee must not ever have seen that one, either. She cut across the grass and ran up to Louis, the yard teacher.

"I want a green ball," Deedee said. The green balls were the best.

"I'm all out of green balls," said Louis.

"Okay, then I want a red ball," said Deedee. The red balls were just about as good as the green balls. They didn't **bounce** as high, but actually, sometimes you don't want a ball to bounce too high.

"I'm all out of red balls, too," said Louis.

"Do you have anything left?" asked Deedee.

Deedee meant anything **besides** the yellow ball. There was one yellow ball at Wayside School and Louis was always trying to **get rid of** it. It didn't bounce, and it never went the way it was kicked.

"Anything at all?" asked Deedee.

"Today is your lucky day," said Louis. "I have one ball left, just for you; the one and only yellow ball!"

"No, thanks," said Deedee.

"Aw, come on, take it," said Louis.

"Why don't you ever have any green or red balls?" asked Deedee.

"I do," said Louis. "But the other children ask first. By the time you get out here, they're all gone."

"But that's because I have to come **all the way** from the thirtieth **story**. How do you **expect** me to **compete** with the kids from the first or second?" she asked.

"That's why I saved you the yellow ball," said Louis. "Everybody wanted it, but I saved it just for you."

"**I bet**," said Deedee.

She took the yellow ball and bounced it on the ground. It **stop**ped **dead** with a **thud**. She stepped back, ran up, and kicked it. It went **backwards** over her head. She didn't **bother chasing** it.

Instead she played hopscotch with Jennie and Leslie. She thought it was **disgust**ing.

The next day, Deedee asked Mrs. Jewls if she could go to recess early.

"Why?" asked Mrs. Jewls.

"So I can get a green ball before Louis gives them all away," said Deedee.

"I'm glad you have a good reason," said Mrs. Jewls. "Yes, you may go. But first, spell *Mississippi* for me."

Spelling was not Deedee's best **subject**. By the time she finally got it right, she was five minutes late for recess.

She jumped down the stairs, cut across the grass, and ran up to Louis. There were no green balls left. There were no red balls left, either. However, there was still the yellow ball.

Deedee played jump rope[1] with Joy and Maurecia. It was no better than hopscotch.

So Deedee's problem was to **figure out** a way to get a green ball, or at least a red ball.

You already know that this story also contains a solution. Deedee figured it out. See if you can, too. Remember everything you know about Deedee, Wayside School, and Mrs. Jewls.

Hint: The next day, Deedee brought a cream cheese and jelly sandwich, some nuts, and **shred**ded cheese in her **lunchbox**.

Here's what happened.

Just before recess, Deedee **smear**ed the cream cheese and jelly all over her face. Then she **stuff**ed her mouth with nuts and hung the shredded cheese from her nose. When she closed her eyes, she looked just like a dead rat.

Todd was in on the plan. "Mrs. Jewls," he called. "There's a dead rat in the classroom."

Mrs. Jewls was very **put out**. "I want that dead rat outside **immediate**ly!"

When Mrs. Jewls said *immediately*, she meant it. Deedee **instant**ly found herself outside on the **playground**.

"I want a green ball," she said.

Louis **pretend**ed that he hadn't heard her.

"May I *please* have a green ball?" asked Deedee.

---

1   jump rope 줄넘기.

Louis gave her a green ball. "I don't know how you did it, Deedee, but you're first today," he said.

When Mrs. Jewls found out that Deedee and Todd had **trick**ed her, she sent Todd home early on the **kindergarten** bus.

Deedee threw the green ball on the ground. It bounced fifty feet straight up in the air, and then she caught it.

"You don't like me, do you?" she asked Louis.

"Sure I do," said Louis.

"No, you don't," said Deedee.

"Yes, I like you," said Louis.

"No, you don't," Deedee **insist**ed.

"Yes, I like you. I really do," said Louis.

"Are you sure?" asked Deedee.

"Yes," said Louis. "Don't you believe me?"

"I guess so," said Deedee.

"Do you like me?" asked Louis.

"**You bet**," said Deedee. "You're my best friend!"

"**Terrific**," said Louis. "I always wanted to be best friends with a dead rat."

16. D.J.

D.J. **skip**ped up the thirty **flights of stairs** to Mrs. Jewls's room. He was **grin**ning from ear to ear, from nose to **chin**, from here to there, and back again.

"Hey, D.J.," Todd shouted, "glad to see you." Todd was a **pushover** for smiling faces.

Mrs. Jewls heard him. She began to write Todd's name on the board under DISCIPLINE, but when she saw D.J.'s smile, she put down the **chalk**. "Good morning, D.J.," she said. "What are you so happy about?"

D.J. grinned and **shrug**ged his shoulders.

Mrs. Jewls smiled.

Dameon looked at the smile on Mrs. Jewls's face, then at Todd's, and finally at D.J.'s. Then Dameon smiled, too. His smile was almost as big as D.J.'s. They were best friends.

Once they saw the two of them smiling, the rest of the class couldn't help but smile. Rondi had a very cute one, due to her two missing front teeth. Nobody had an ugly smile.

Jason came to school late. He was very upset. But the first thing he saw was Dameon's smile, and he felt a little bit better. Then he saw Rondi's **toothless** grin, and he even began to smile a little himself. But when he saw the piano on D.J.'s face, he fell, laughing, onto the floor.

Everybody started to laugh, even Kathy, and she **hardly** ever laughed except when someone hurt himself.

The whole room seemed to be laughing, not just the people in it. The blackboard **chuckle**d. The **ceiling snicker**ed. The desks were jumping up and down, and the chairs were **slap**ping one another on the back. The floor was very **ticklish**. It laughed until the walls turned purple. The **wastepaper** basket started to sing, and all the pencils stood up and danced.

Finally things began to **settle down**. Mrs. Jewls **wipe**d her eyes and said, "D.J., why don't you tell the class why you are so happy? At least let us know what we are laughing about."

But D.J. just kept on smiling.

"Aw, come on, D.J.," said Deedee. "Tell us."

D.J. didn't say a word. He couldn't. His mouth was **stretched out of shape**.

"Let us guess," said Ron. "If we guess right, will you tell us?"

D.J. **nod**ded his head. His smile began to hurt his ears.

Everyone took one guess.

"Have you been swimming?"

"Is it your birthday?"

"Are you in love?"

"Did you get a green ball?"

Nobody guessed right.

At recess D.J. was still smiling.

Louis, the yard teacher, called, "Hey, D.J. Come here."

They walked to the far corner of the playground, where they were alone.

"What's up, D.J.?" Louis asked.

D.J. just smiled.

"Come on, D.J. You can tell me. Why are you so happy?"

D.J. looked up at him. He said, "You need a reason to be sad. You don't need a reason to be happy."

17. JOHN

John had light brown hair and a round head. He was Joe's best friend. John was one of the smartest boys in Mrs. Jewls's class. But he had one problem. He could only read words written **upside down**.

Nobody ever wrote anything upside down.

But it was only a little problem. John was still in the high reading group. He just turned his book upside down.

It was easier for John to turn his book upside down than to learn to read **correct**ly. But the easiest way isn't always the best way.

Mrs. Jewls said, "John, you can't go on reading like this. You can't **spend** the rest of your life turning your books upside down."

"Why not?" asked John.

"Because I said so," said Mrs. Jewls. "**Besides**, what happens when I write something on the blackboard? You can't turn the blackboard upside down."

"No, I guess you're right," said John.

"I know I'm right," said Mrs. Jewls. "You are going to have to learn to **stand** on your head."

John couldn't stand on his head. He had **given up** trying. You would have, too, if you had fallen over as many times as he had.

Joe was John's best friend. He could stand on John's head. Every time John fell over, Joe stood on his head. **After all**, what are best friends for?

"My head is too round, Mrs. Jewls. I can't stand on it," said John.

"Of course you can, John," said Mrs. Jewls. "If Joe can stand on your head, so can you."

"It's easy, John," said Joe.

"I can't," John repeated. "I always fall over."

"**Nonsense**," said Mrs. Jewls. "All you have to do is find your center of balance. Now, up you go."

John put his round head on the floor and **swung** his legs up. He fell right over. Then Joe stood on John's head.

"See, John, it's easy. **Nothing to it**," Joe said.

"We'll help you, John," said Mrs. Jewls. "Joe, get off John's head and get me the **pillow** from under my desk. Nancy, Calvin, come here and **give** us **a hand**."

Mrs. Jewls took the pillow from Joe and set it on the floor. "All right, John, we'll **surround** you," she said. "We won't let you fall."

John put his head on the pillow and swung his legs up. He started to fall one way, but Nancy pushed him back up. Then he started to fall another way, but Calvin **straighten**ed him out. John kept falling a little bit this way and that way until at last he found his center of balance.

"Hey, look at me. Look at me," said John. "I'm up. I'm really up. I'm standing on my head. I found my center of balance. It's beautiful. I can read the blackboard! Hey, Calvin, bring me a book, and you don't have to turn it upside down. Ha Ha. Hey, who, aaaaahhhh. . . ."

BAMM!! While Calvin went to get the book, John fell flat on his face.

"You better stay off my head, Joe," he **warn**ed.

"Are you all right, John?" asked Mrs. Jewls.

"Yes, I think so. I feel a little funny. Hey! I can still read the blackboard, and I'm not upside down. I can read right side up now. When I fell, I must have **flip**ped my brain or something."

"That is wonderful, John," said Mrs. Jewls. "Here, put the

pillow back under my desk. As a **reward** you may have a Tootsie Roll pop. They are in the coffee can on top of my desk."

John placed the pillow on top of her desk. Then he looked under the desk, but he couldn't find the Tootsie Roll pops anywhere.

18. LESLIE

Leslie had five fingers on each hand and five toes on each foot. For each hand she had an arm, and for each foot she had a leg. She was a very lucky girl. And she had two lovely, long brown **pigtail**s that reached all the way down to her waist.

When Mrs. Jewls asked a question, Leslie could raise one of her hands.

When Leslie was adding, she could **count** on her fingers.

When Paul pulled one of her pigtails, she could kick him with one foot while standing on the other.

But Leslie had one problem. She didn't know what to do with

her toes. She had ten **adorable** little toes and nothing to do with them. As far as she could tell, they **served** no **useful** purpose.

"**Suck** your toes. That's what I do," said Sharie.

But Leslie's foot wouldn't reach her mouth.

"Well, that's all toes are good for," said Sharie. She put her foot in her mouth and went to sleep.

"No," thought Leslie. "They must be good for something. They just have to be."

During **recess**, she asked Dana. "Dana, what do you do with your toes?"

"I **scratch** the back of my legs," said Dana. "First I scratch my left leg with my right foot. Then I scratch my right leg with my left foot."

"But my legs don't **itch**," said Leslie.

"That's good," said Dana. "In that case you can scratch my legs. With your help I can scratch both legs at the same time."

"No, never mind," said Leslie. She walked up behind Louis, the **yard** teacher, and **hop**ped on his shoulders.

"Louis," said Leslie. "I don't know what to do with my toes."

Louis **tug**ged her foot. "Yes, that is a serious problem," he said, "but I'll tell you what I'll do. I'll **take** them **off your hands** for you, or rather, your feet. Just cut them off and give them to me."

"What?" asked Leslie.

"You don't want them, so I'll take them," said Louis. "You

won't have to worry about them ever again."

"No," said Leslie.

"I'll give them to Miss Mush," said Louis. "She can make little hot dogs[1] out of them." Miss Mush was the lunch teacher.

"No, I'm not going to give my toes away," said Leslie.

"All right," said Louis. "I'll give you a **nickel apiece** for them."

"No, you can't have them," said Leslie.

"Why not?" Louis asked. "They're no good to you, **anyhow.** And think of all you can buy for fifty cents."

The bell rang.

"I'll **think** it **over,**" said Leslie. She ran back to class.

"Mrs. Jewls," said Leslie, "I don't see any reason for keeping my toes."

"Oh, Leslie, I'm sure there are lots of good reasons," said Mrs. Jewls.

"Well, I can't think of any. My legs don't itch, and I can't get my foot in my mouth. Louis **offer**ed me a nickel apiece for them, and it seems to me like a good deal. But I wanted to check with you first."

"I think Louis was **pull**ing **your leg,**" said Mrs. Jewls.

"No," said Leslie, "he was pulling my toes."

"What would he want with your toes?" asked Mrs. Jewls.

"I don't know," said Leslie, "but if he's willing to give me

---

1 hot dog 핫도그. 긴 빵에 소시지를 끼워서 먹는 음식.

five cents apiece for them, then I'm going to **take** him **up on** it. That's fifty cents."

At lunch, Leslie walked up to Louis. "Okay, Louis," she said, "you can have my toes for a nickel apiece. That will be fifty cents."

"Not so fast," said Louis, "Let me look at them first."

Leslie took off her shoes.

"Yes, yes," said Louis, "the big ones are good, and the ones next to them, but the most I'll give you for the rest of your toes is three cents each."

Leslie was **furious**. "Three cents each! You told me five at recess."

"I'll give you five cents for the big ones. But just look at that **scrawny** little **runt** of a toe on the end, there. You're lucky to be getting even three cents for it. I think you're getting a darn good deal."

"I happen to like that toe," said Leslie.

"Fine, then," said Louis, "keep it. I'll just take the two big toes, and we'll **call it square**." He reached in his pocket and pulled out a **dime**.

"**Nothing doing**," said Leslie. "These toes are sold as a set. It's either all ten for fifty cents or no deal. What am I going to do with just eight toes?"

"Then **forget it**," said Louis. "I'm not going to give you a nickel for those scrawny little end toes."

"Fine," said Leslie, "no deal. My toes will still be here if you change your mind." She turned and walked toward the hopscotch area.

"Wait a second," Louis called. "I'll give you a dollar each for your pigtails."

Leslie turned around and looked at him with **fiery** eyes. "Cut my hair!" she **exclaim**ed. "Are you crazy?"

19. MISS ZARVES

There is no Miss Zarves. There is no nineteenth story. Sorry.

20. KATHY

Kathy doesn't like you. She doesn't know you, but she still doesn't like you. She thinks you are stupid! In fact, she thinks you are the stupidest person she doesn't know. What do you think of that?

She also thinks you're ugly! As a **matter** of fact, she thinks you are the ugliest person she doesn't know. And she doesn't know a lot of people.

She doesn't like the people she knows, either. She hates everybody in Mrs. Jewls's class. She did like one member of the class. She liked Sammy. She thought he was funny. Sammy was a dead rat.

But Kathy has good reasons for not liking any of the children she knows. She doesn't like D.J. because he smiles too much, and she doesn't like John because he can't stand on his head.

Kathy once had a cat named Skunks. She liked Skunks. But she was afraid that Skunks would **run away**.

"You have nothing to worry about, Kathy," said Mrs. Jewls. "Skunks won't run away. Just be nice to him and **feed** him and **pet** him, and he won't run away. He may go out and play, but he'll always come back."

"No, you're wrong, Mrs. Jewls," said Kathy. "What do you know! He'll run away."

So Kathy kept Skunks **lock**ed up in her **closet** at home. She never let him out and sometimes even forgot to feed him.

One day, while Kathy was looking for her other shoe, Skunks ran out of the closet and never came back.

"You said he would come back, Mrs. Jewls," said Kathy. "He never came back. You were wrong. I was right."

That was why Kathy didn't like Mrs. Jewls.

"The next time I get a cat, I'll kill him. Then he'll never run away," said Kathy.

Then there was the time that Dameon tried to teach Kathy how to play **catch**.

Dameon said, "When I throw you the ball, Kathy, try to catch it."

"I can't catch it," said Kathy. "I'll just get hurt."

"You won't get hurt," Dameon **insist**ed. "Just watch the ball."
He **toss**ed it to her.

But Kathy knew she'd get hurt. So she closed her eyes. The ball hit her on the **cheek**. It hurt.

Kathy began to cry. "You were wrong," she **sob**bed. "I was right!"

That was why Kathy didn't like Dameon.

Allison believed that if you are nice to someone, then they'll be nice to you. So one day she brought Kathy a cookie.

"I don't want your ugly cookie," said Kathy. "It probably tastes **terrible!**"

Allison said, "No, it is very good. I made it myself."

Kathy said, "If you made it, then it must **stink**! You can't cook. You're too stupid!" She just put the cookie in her desk along with her pencils, **crayon**s, and books.

Three weeks later, Kathy was hungry. "All right, Allison," she said. "I'll try your stupid cookie."

She took it out of her desk. It was **cover**ed with **dust**. She **bit** it. It was hard and tasted terrible.

"See," said Kathy. "I was right!"

That was why Kathy didn't like Allison.

Yes, Kathy had very good reasons for not liking anybody she knew.

But she also has a good reason for not liking you. And she doesn't even know you. Her reason is this. She knows that if you ever met her, you wouldn't like her. You don't like Kathy, do you?

See, she was right!

It's funny how a person can be right all the time and still be wrong.

21. RON

Ron had **curly** hair and little feet. "I want to play **kickball**," he said.

"You can't play," said Terrence.

"Get out of here," said Deedee.

"**Scram**," said Jason.

"I want to play kickball," said Ron.

"Well, you're not playing," said Terrence. "**Beat it**!"

Ron **stomp**ed across the **playground** to the hopscotch area. Jenny was playing hopscotch with Louis. Jenny was on nine. Louis was still on four, but it was his turn.

"I want to play kickball," Ron said.

"So, go play kickball," said Louis.

"Terrence won't let me play," said Ron.

Louis walked with Ron to the kickball **field**.

"Hey, what about our hopscotch game?" Jenny asked.

"You won," said Louis.

"I just **beat** Louis in hopscotch!" Jenny **announce**d. Leslie, Rondi, and Allison **flock**ed around her.

"Hey, Louis," Dameon shouted. "Do you want to play kickball?"

"All right," said Louis. "Ron and I will both play."

"No," said Terrence. "Ron isn't playing."

"Anyone who wants to play can play," said Louis.

"No, he can't," said Terrence. "It's my ball."

"It isn't your ball," said Louis.

"You gave it to me," said Terrence.

"I gave it to you to share," said Louis. "If you can't share it, you can't have it."

"Oh, all right," said Terrence. "But I get to **pitch**."

"Ron and I will **stand** everybody!" Louis announced.

"All right!" said Jason. "We'll kill them!"

"We'll **murder** them!" said Deedee.

"We'll **smash** them!" said Myron.

"We'll see," said Louis.

Ron pitched, and Louis played the other eight **position**s. Twenty minutes later, they finally got three outs.[1] The score was twenty-one to nothing.

Ron was up first.

"**Infield** in!" shouted Dameon. Everybody stood within ten feet of **home plate**.

"All right, Ron," Louis shouted, "kick it over their heads!"

Ron kicked the ball only three-and-a-half feet. Todd picked it up and threw him out.

Louis was up. Everybody ran back to the edge of the **outfield**. Still, Louis kicked the ball over their heads for a home run.

Everybody ran **all the way** back in again for Ron's up. He kicked the ball only two feet. Deedee **tag**ged him **out**.

Louis kicked another home run.

Ron then kicked the ball a foot and **trip**ped over it on his way to first base. Three outs.

Ron and Louis held the other team to only five runs the next **inning**. That was because the bell rang. Lunch was finally over.

Louis and Ron lost twenty-six to two. Ron had had a wonderful time.

The next day Ron said, "I want to play kickball."

"You can't play," said Terrence.

"Get out of here," said Jason.

"Scram," said Deedee.

"I want to play kickball," Ron told Louis.

---

1 three outs 삼진 아웃. 야구에서 공격 팀 선수 3명이 아웃된 것을 말한다. 규칙에 따라 공격 팀과 수비 팀의 교대가 이루어진다.

Louis walked with him to the kickball field. "Ron and I will stand all of you."

Everybody liked the teams.

Ron pitched while Louis played the other eight positions. They lost fifty-seven to two.

After the game Louis took Ron aside. "Listen. Ron," he said, "why do you always want to play kickball? You can't kick. You can't field. You can't even run to first base. You just get smashed every game."

"Hey, now wait a second," said Ron. "Don't go **blaming** it all on me. You're half the team, too, you know." And with that, he **punch**ed Louis in the **stomach**.

And he punched a heck[2] of a lot harder than he kicked.

---

2 heck 'hell'을 완곡하게 표현한 말로, '젠장'이라는 뜻이다. 여기서처럼 'a heck of'로 쓰이는 경우에는 '대단한' 또는 '엄청난'이라고 해석할 수 있다.

22. THE THREE ERICS

In Mrs. Jewls's class there were three children named Eric: Eric Fry, Eric Bacon, and Eric Ovens. They were known **throughout** the school for being fat. Eric Fry sat at this end of the room. Eric Bacon sat in the middle of the room. And Eric Ovens sat at that end of the room. There was a joke around Wayside School that if all three Erics were ever at the same end of the room at the same time, the whole school would **tip** over.

Eric Bacon hated jokes like that. That's not surprising. **After all**, he wasn't even fat. In fact, he was the **skinniest** kid in Mrs. Jewls's class. But nobody seemed to **notice**. The other two Erics were fat, and so everyone just thought that all Erics were fat.

"But I'm not fat!" Eric Bacon **insist**ed.

"What's your name?" asked Jason.

"Eric," said Eric Bacon.

"Then you're fat," Jason **conclude**d.

And pretty soon, skinny little Eric Bacon, the skinniest kid in Mrs. Jewls's class, had the **nickname** "Fatso.[1]"

Eric Fry really *was* fat. He was also the best **athlete** in Mrs. Jewls's class. His body was **solid muscle**. However, nobody ever noticed.

The other two Erics weren't very good at **sport**s. Eric Ovens was **clumsy**. Eric ("Fatso") Bacon was a good athlete for his size, but because he was so skinny he didn't have much power.

So, naturally, everybody just **assume**d that Eric Fry was also clumsy and weak. After all, his name *was* Eric.

Whenever the other kids chose up teams, Eric Fry was the last one picked. They never noticed his home runs or the **fabulous** catches he made. Like all great athletes, he made the impossible look easy. Of course, the other kids did notice the one time that he dropped the ball.

Eric Fry was playing right field. Terrence **belt**ed a deep fly[2] to left. Eric Fry **race**d all the way across the field after the ball

---

1 fatso 뚱뚱보.
2 fly 플라이. 타자가 공중으로 쳐서 올린 공.

and at the last second dived at it. He caught it in **midair** on his **fingertip**s, but as he hit the ground the ball **squirt**ed loose.

"Well, what do you **expect** from 'Butterfingers,[3]'" said Stephen.

And since that time Eric Fry has had the nickname "Butterfingers."

Eric Ovens was the nicest person in Mrs. Jewls's class. He **treat**ed everyone **equal**ly and always had a kind word to say. But because his name was Eric, everyone thought he was mean.

"Fatso" was mean because everyone called him "Fatso."

"Butterfingers" was mean because he always had to play right field.

So, naturally, everyone just assumed that Eric Ovens was also mean. They called him "Crabapple.[4]"

"Good morning, Allison," said Eric Ovens. "How are you?"

"**Lay off**, 'Crabapple'! Will ya?" answered Allison. "If you don't have something nice to say, don't say anything at all."

All three of the Erics had nicknames. It was better that way. **Otherwise** when someone said, "Hey, Eric," no one knew to whom he was talking. One time all the Erics would answer, and the next time none of them would answer. But when someone said, "Hey, 'Crabapple,'" then Eric Ovens knew they were talking to him. And if someone said, "Hey, 'Butterfingers,'" Eric Fry knew

---

3 butterfingers 손에 든 물건을 잘 떨어뜨리는 사람.
4 crabapple '성질이 비뚤어진 사람'을 가리키는 구어.

they meant him. And when someone said, "Hey, 'Fatso,'" Eric Bacon knew that he was being called.

23. ALLISON

Allison had pretty **blonde** hair and always wore a sky-blue **windbreaker**. Her windbreaker was the same color as her eyes. She was best friends with Rondi. Rondi had blonde hair, too, but she was missing her two front teeth. Allison had all of her teeth.

Allison used to say that she **knock**ed Rondi's teeth out. Allison was very pretty, so all the boys in Mrs. Jewls's class **tease**d her, especially Jason. But Allison said, "Leave me alone or I'll knock your teeth out—like I did Rondi's." The boys didn't **bother** her after that.

One day Allison brought a tangerine[1] for lunch. She took

the **peel** off in one piece.

Miss Mush, the lunch teacher, walked up to her. "Allison, may I have your tangerine?" she asked.

Miss Mush always gave food to the children. So Allison was happy to give her tangerine to Miss Mush.

Miss Mush **shove**d it in her mouth and **swallow**ed it in less than four seconds.

Allison left the **lunchroom** and walked down to the library. The lunchroom was on the fifteenth **story**. The library was on the seventh. Allison already had her book. She just went to the library because it was nice and quiet there.

The **librarian** walked up to Allison. "What are you reading?" she asked.

Allison told her the name of the book.

"That sounds like a good book," said the librarian. "I never read that one. May I borrow it?"

The librarian always lent books to the children. Allison was glad to be able to return the **favor**. She gave the librarian the book, then walked down the stairs, outside to the playground.

All of Allison's friends were playing **freeze tag**.[2] Allison didn't feel like playing. She reached into the pocket of her sky-blue windbreaker and took out a tennis ball. She **bounce**d it a couple

---

1 tangerine 감귤.
2 freeze tag 얼음 땡 놀이.

of times on the ground.

Louis came up to her. "Hi, Allison," he said. "May I play with your tennis ball?"

Louis always gave balls to the children. Allison happily gave her ball to Louis.

Louis threw the ball all the way to the other side of the playground. Then he went **chasing** after it.

Allison didn't feel like doing anything. Jason ran up and tagged her.

"You're frozen," he said.

"Get out of here before I knock your teeth out," said Allison.

Jason **shrug**ged his shoulders and left.

Allison went back inside and up the thirty **flights of stairs** to Mrs. Jewls's room. The lunch **period** wasn't over yet, but Allison didn't feel like doing anything else. She had given her food to the lunch teacher, her book to the librarian, and her ball to the **yard** teacher. She went inside her classroom.

Mrs. Jewls was there. "Oh, Allison, I'm glad you're here," said Mrs. Jewls. "I'm having trouble with an **arithmetic** problem. Maybe you can help."

"Sure," said Allison. Mrs. Jewls always helped the children with their problems. Allison was happy to help.

"How do you **spell** *chair*?" asked Mrs. Jewls.

"C-H-A-I-R," said Allison.

"Yes, that's right," said Mrs. Jewls. "I knew it wasn't C-H-A-

R-E, but I couldn't remember what it was."

"That's not an arithmetic problem," said Allison. "That's spelling."

"Yes, you are right again," said Mrs. Jewls. "I always get the two **mixed up**."

The bell rang. The lunch period was over. Allison could hear the other children running up the stairs.

"Allison," said Mrs. Jewls. "You learned a very important secret today, and I don't want you to tell any of the other children, not even Rondi."

"What was that?" asked Allison. She didn't even know she had learned a secret. She loved secrets.

"You learned that children are really smarter than their teachers," said Mrs. Jewls.

"Oh, that's no secret," said Allison. "Everybody knows that."

24. DAMEON

Dameon had **hazel** eyes with a little black **dot** in the middle of each of them. The dots were called **pupils**. So was Dameon. He was a pupil in Mrs. Jewls's class.

Mrs. Jewls was about to show the class a movie. She **turn**ed **out** the lights. When it was dark, Dameon's pupils got bigger.

"Dameon," said Mrs. Jewls, "run **downstairs** and ask Louis if he'd like to see the movie with us."

Dameon ran down the thirty flights of stairs to the **playground**. He stepped outside as Louis was **hook**ing up a tetherball.[1]

"Hey, Louis," Dameon called. "Do you want to see a movie

in Mrs. Jewls's class?"

Louis **rub**bed his **chin**. "What movie?" he asked.

Dameon **shrug**ged his shoulders. "I don't know," he said. "I'll be right back."

Dameon ran **all the way** back up the stairs to the thirtieth story.

"Louis wants to know, what movie?" said Dameon.

"Does he want to know the name of the movie or what the movie is about?" asked Mrs. Jewls.

"I don't know, said Dameon. "I'll ask him."

Dameon raced back down the stairs and out to the playground.

"Louis, do you want to know the name of the movie or what the movie is about?" he asked.

"The name," said Louis.

"Okay," said Dameon.

Dameon hurried back up the thirty flights of stairs. He took the steps two at a time.

"He wants to know the name," said Dameon.

"*Turtles*," said Mrs. Jewls.

Dameon turned around, took a deep breath, then ran back down the stairs.

"*Turtles*," Dameon told Louis.

"Hey, that might be good," said Louis. "What's it about?"

---

1 tetherball 테더 볼. 기둥에 매단 공을 치고 받는 게임. 이 게임에 쓰이는 공을 가리키기도 한다.

"I'm not sure," said Dameon. "I'll find out."

Dameon raced back up the stairs. But first he stopped to take a drink of water.

"What's it about, Mrs. Jewls?" asked Dameon.

"Turtles," said Mrs. Jewls.

Dameon **rush**ed back down the stairs to tell Louis.

"Turtles," said Dameon.

"No, thanks," said Louis. "I don't like turtles. They are too slow."

Dameon lowered his head and slowly walked up the thirty flights of stairs. His legs were **sore**, he could **hardly** breathe, and his **side ache**d.

By the time he got to Mrs. Jewls's class, the movie was over.

"All right, class," said Mrs. Jewls. "I want everybody to take out a piece of paper and a pencil and write something about turtles."

Dameon had missed the movie, but he still could have written something about turtles: "Turtles are too slow." But now he couldn't find his pencil. It just wasn't his day.

"What's the **matter**, Dameon?" asked Mrs. Jewls.

"I can't find my pencil," said Dameon.

"Class, Dameon's pencil is missing," Mrs. Jewls announced. "What did it look like, Dameon?" she asked.

"It was long and yellow," said Dameon. "It had a black point at one end and a red **eraser** at the other."

"I found it," said Todd, "here, by the **blackboard**."

"Yes, that's it," said Dameon.

"No, there it is, in the corner by the **waste** basket," said "Crabapple."

"Hmmm, maybe that's it," said Dameon.

"Here it is," said John. "It's been in my desk the whole time."

"No, here it is in my hand," said Joe.

"I found it," said Rondi.

"Here it is," said Allison.

"I have it," laughed D.J.

"I found it," said Myron.

"Which one is yours, Dameon?" asked Mrs. Jewls.

Dameon studied each pencil. "They all look like mine," he said.

Fortunately, at that moment, Louis walked into the classroom. He **hand**ed Dameon a pencil.

"You dropped this when you were telling me about the movie," said Louis.

"Thanks," said Dameon.

"Okay, class," said Mrs. Jewls. "So that we have no more **mix-up**s, I want everybody to write his name on his pencil."

Dameon **spent** the rest of the day trying to write his name on his pencil.

Dameon's pencil couldn't write on itself. It was just like his beautiful hazel eyes with the black dots in the middle. They could see everything except themselves.

25. JENNY

Jenny came to school on the back of her father's **motorcycle**. She was late. Wayside School began at nine o'clock. It was almost nine-thirty. She kissed her father good-bye and raced up the thirty **flights of stairs** to Mrs. Jewls's room.

"I'm sorry I'm late, Mrs. Jewls, but my father's motorcycle lost a. . . ." There was nobody there.

The room was empty.

"Hello, hello," she cried. "Mrs. Jewls, Dana, Todd, anyone?"

There was no one in the room.

"Maybe I'm early," Jenny thought. She looked up at the clock.

It was **exactly** nine-thirty.

"Oh, I hope they didn't go on a **field trip** without me." She looked out the window. Nobody was there, not even Louis.

Jenny didn't know what to do. She sat down at her desk. She watched the second hand[1] go around on the clock. "I might as well **catch up** on my **spell**ing," she thought. She opened her desk and took out her speller.

M-U-D spells *mud*.

"Where is everybody?"

B-L-O-O-D spells *blood*.

"I hope nothing happened to them."

B-L-A-C-K spells *black*.

Jenny heard **footstep**s coming down the hall. She began to work very fast.

H-A-C-K spells ***hack***. S-M-A-C-K spells ***smack***. Someone opened the door. Jenny turned around. "Ack!" she **gasp**ed.

He was a man Jenny had never seen before. He had a black **mustache** and a matching **attaché case**.

Jenny jumped out of her seat.

"Get back in your seat," the man said.

Jenny slowly sat down.

The man walked over and sat down in Dana's seat, facing Jenny. He opened his attaché case and **remove**d some papers.

---

1   second hand 시계의 초침.

106

"What is your name?" he asked her.

"Jenny," Jenny **whisper**ed.

"Jenny?" the man repeated as if he didn't believe her.

"Well, it is actually Jennifer, Jenny for short," said Jenny.

"I see," said the man. He took the speller from Jenny's desk. Jenny's name was written across the top. He put the speller in his attaché case.

"What are you doing here, Jennifer?" he asked.

"This is my classroom," said Jenny.

"Are you sure?" the man asked.

"Yes, I think so. I mean—"

"Where is the rest of your class?" the man asked.

"I don't know," said Jenny, "maybe they went on a field trip."

"No," said the man. "They didn't go on a field trip."

"Well, I don't know where they are!" Jenny cried. "I was half an hour late today, and when I got here everybody was gone. Really! Did something happen to them?"

The man didn't answer her. He wrote something on a piece of paper. "Tell me something, Jennifer. When you came to school today and saw that nobody was here, weren't you somewhat **puzzle**d?"

"Yes. Yes," said Jenny. "What happened to them?"

"If you are really so **concern**ed and so puzzled," said the man, "why did you work on spelling?"

"I don't know," said Jenny.

"It would seem to me," the man said, "that if a child came to school and nobody was there, she might play games, or walk around, or go home, but **certain**ly not work on spelling."

Jenny started to cry. "I didn't know what to do. I was late and had to **ride** on a motorcycle and nobody was here and now you are asking me all kinds of questions and I'm afraid of what has happened to Dana and Mrs. Jewls and Rondi and Allison."

The man didn't understand a word she said.

Jenny heard more footsteps. The man got up and opened the door. Two more men came in. One had a black mustache like the first man. The other man was **bald**.

Jenny was **frighten**ed by them.

"Does she know?" asked the **newcomer** with the mustache.

"She **claim**s she knows nothing," the first man answered. "She says she was late today, and when she got here everybody was gone."

"Do you believe her?" asked the man with the bald head.

"I'm not sure. She was working on her speller when I walked in." He reached into his attaché case and took out Jenny's speller. He **hand**ed it to the man with the bald head.

The bald man read Jenny's name across the top of it. "Tell me, Jenny," he said, "why are you the only one here?"

"I don't know," said Jenny.

"Has this ever happened before?" he asked.

"No, never," said Jenny.

He gave Jenny her speller. "Put this inside your desk."

Jenny put it away.

"I'm **satisfied**," said the man with the bald head.

"Okay, Jennifer," said the first man, "you may go now."

Jenny got out of her seat.

"Jenny," the bald man called.

Jenny turned slowly around. "Yes?" she whispered.

"Next time, don't come to school on a Saturday.

26. TERRENCE

Terrence was a good **athlete** but a bad **sport**.

Rondi and Allison were playing two-square[1] with a red ball.

"Can I play?" asked Terrence.

"No," Allison **replied**.

"You have to let me play," Terrence said. "Louis says we have to share the balls."

"Well, we're not sharing with you," said Allison.

---

1   two-square 두 사람이 하는 four-square 게임. four-square는 네 사람이 네 개의 정사각형으로 이루어진 코트의 각 모서리에 서서 서로 공을 주고 받는 게임을 말한다.

"Oh, let him play," said Rondi.

"All right," said Allison. "We'll play three-square.[2] You better play right."

"I will," said Terrence.

Allison **bounce**d the ball to Rondi. Rondi bounced it over to Terrence. Terrence caught it and kicked it over the **fence**.

"You have to go get it," said Allison.

"Shut up, Dixie cup,[3]" Terrence answered.

Rondi ran and told Louis.

D.J. and Dameon were playing basketball. "Uh-oh, here comes Terrence," said Dameon.

"Hey, let me play," said Terrence.

"**Get lost**, Terrence," said Dameon.

"You have to share the balls. Louis says so," said Terrence.

"Okay, but just throw it in the basket. Don't kick it," said Dameon.

"I won't," said Terrence.

First Dameon **took a shot**. It bounced off the backboard and through the **hoop**.

Next D.J. took a shot. He threw it **underhand**, **way** up in the air. It came down through the hoop without touching the **rim**.

---

2   three-square 세 사람이 하는 four-square 게임을 말한다.
3   Dixie cup 딕시 컵. 원래는 종이컵의 상품명이었지만, 종이컵을 뜻하는 일반명사처럼 쓰인다.

Then Terrence took a shot. He kicked it over the fence.

"You **idiot**," said Dameon.

"Take a train, peanut brain," Terrence answered.

D.J. went and told Louis.

Stephen, Calvin, Joe, John, and Leslie were playing spud.[4] Stephen was IT.[5] Everyone else had a number. Stephen had to throw the ball up in the air and call out a number. The person who had that number had to try to catch it.

"Can I play?" asked Terrence.

"No," said Calvin. "You'll just kick the ball over the fence."

"No," said Joe.

"**No way**," said John.

"No," said Leslie.

"Sure," said Stephen. "**Newcomer**s are IT.[5]" He gave the ball to Terrence. "Just throw the ball up in the air and call out a number between one and five."

"Okay," said Terrence.

The children formed a circle around Terrence.

"A million," **yell**ed Terrence as he kicked the ball over the fence.

"What did you do that for?" asked Stephen.

---

4   spud 스퍼드. 술래가 공을 위로 높이 던지면서 숫자를 외치면, 술래를 빙 둘러싼 채 떨어
    져서 서 있던 사람 중 그 숫자에 해당되는 참여자가 그 공을 받아야 하는 게임이다. 부르
    는 숫자는 1부터 게임에 참여하는 전체 인원수 사이에서 선택할 수 있다.

5   it 놀이의 술래.

112

"Eat a frog, **warthog**," said Terrence.

Stephen ran and told Louis.

Terrence looked around. There was nothing to do. There were no balls left.

Louis walked up to him. He was followed by Allison, Rondi, Dameon, D.J., Stephen, Calvin, Joe, John, and Leslie.

"What's the matter, Terrence?" asked Louis.

"There are no balls," said Terrence. "Do you have a green ball?"

"No," said Louis. "All of my balls have **mysterious**ly disappeared."

"Darn it," said Terrence. "There is nothing left to kick."

"Nothing left to kick?" asked Louis. "Oh, I don't know about that. What do you think, Rondi? Is there anything left to kick?"

Rondi thought a minute. Then she smiled. She was missing her two front teeth. "Yes, there is something left to kick," she said.

"Well where is it?" asked Terrence.

"Let me check with Allison," said Louis. "Allison, is there anything left to kick?" He winked at her.

"There sure is," said Allison.

"What, what?" asked Terrence.

"How about you, Dameon?" asked Louis. "Can you think of anything?"

Dameon **nod**ded his head yes.

"Well, what is it?" asked Terrence. He couldn't wait.

"D.J., we got anything around here to kick?" asked Louis.

D.J. smiled. "Yes, we do," he said.

"Give it to me. Give it to me," Terrence **demand**ed.

"I don't know if I should," said Louis. "What do you think, Calvin? Should I give it to him?"

"I think you should," said Calvin.

"You heard Calvin," said Terrence. "Give it to me."

"Not so fast," said Louis. "Leslie, should I give it to him?"

"Oh, yes, I think he **deserve**s it," said Leslie.

"Give it to me. Give it to me," Terrence repeated.

"Do you also think he deserves it, Joe?" asked Louis.

"Yes, I think so," said Joe.

"What about you, John?" asked Louis.

"**Definite**ly give it to him," John answered.

"**Come on.** Come on," said Terrence. "**Recess** is almost over."

"We'll leave it up to Stephen," said Louis. "Whatever he says goes."

"Let him have it," said Stephen.

"You heard him, Louis," said Terrence. "Let me have it."

"Okay," said Louis.

He picked Terrence up and kicked him over the fence.

27. JOY

Joy had forgotten her lunch at home. It was **lunchtime**. She was hungry.

She didn't have a **meal** ticket. If she had had a meal ticket, she could have had a lunch from Miss Mush, the lunch teacher. She'd have to be **terribly** hungry to eat a lunch made by Miss Mush. Even an empty brown paper **sack** would taste better. But that's how hungry Joy was.

Dameon hadn't forgotten his lunch. He had brought a lovely **turkey** sandwich, a big piece of chocolate cake, and a **crisp**, red apple. All he needed was a glass of milk. He could get that from

Miss Mush. Miss Mush didn't know how to **ruin** milk.

Dameon left his lunch on his desk and went to the end of the milk line.

Joy didn't **waste** any time. She reached into Dameon's sack and took out the apple. But then she **spot**ted the turkey sandwich. She put back the apple, took the sandwich, and **notice**d the chocolate cake. She put back the sandwich and took out the cake.

But then Joy **had second thoughts**. She put back the cake. Then she **grab**bed Dameon's whole lunch.

First she ate the sandwich. It was in a Baggie.[1] When she finished the sandwich, she placed the Baggie on Jason's desk.

Next she ate the chocolate cake. It was **wrap**ped in wax paper.[2] She put the wax paper on Allison's desk.

She ate the apple last. She placed the apple **core** on Deedee's desk.

Then she put the empty sack on Calvin's desk.

Dameon returned with his glass of milk. "Mrs. Jewls, my lunch is gone!" he called.

"I wonder where it could be," said Mrs. Jewls.

"Calvin took it," said Joy. "There's the empty sack on his desk."

"Good work, Joy," said Mrs. Jewls. "Calvin, I'm **ashamed** of you." She wrote Calvin's name on the blackboard under the word

---

1 **baggie** 흔히 지퍼백이라고 부르는 식품용 비닐 주머니.
2 **wax paper** 왁스가 발라져 있어 기름이 스며들지 않는 종이.

DISCIPLINE.

"Look, the Baggie from Dameon's turkey sandwich is on Jason's desk!" Joy called.

"Very good, Joy," said Mrs. Jewls. "But how did you know that Dameon had a turkey sandwich?"

"I'm just smart," said Joy.

Mrs. Jewls wrote Jason's name on the blackboard under Calvin's.

"And there's the wax paper from the delicious chocolate cake on Allison's desk," Joy **announce**d. Joy had chocolate all around her lips.

Allison **stood firm**. She looked into Mrs. Jewls's eyes. "I didn't eat his cake," she said.

"The **evidence** is there on your desk," said Mrs. Jewls. "Joy spotted it." She wrote Allison's name under Jason's.

"Dameon's apple core is on Deedee's desk," said Joy.

"Very good, Joy," said Mrs. Jewls. She wrote Deedee's name under Allison's.

"Dameon, I think you **ought to** thank Joy," said Mrs. Jewls. "She **solve**d the mystery."

"Thank you, Joy," said Dameon.

Just then, Louis, the **yard** teacher, walked in. "I have your lunch, Joy," he said. "Your mother brought it. You left it at home."

"You mean you didn't have a lunch?" asked Mrs. Jewls. "You must be very hungry."

"No," said Joy, "not really. Since Dameon didn't get to eat, he can have it."

"Thanks a lot!" said Dameon. "You are the greatest!"

He ate Joy's lunch, an old bologna sandwich and a **dried-up** carrot.

"Joy, for being such a good **detective**, and for being so **generous** with your lunch, you may **help yourself** to a Tootsie Roll pop," said Mrs. Jewls. "They are in the coffee can on top of my desk."

Joy took one. Then, when Mrs. Jewls wasn't looking, she took another.

Calvin, Jason, Allison, and Deedee had their names on the blackboard under the word DISCIPLINE. But they were good the rest of the day, so at two o'clock Mrs. Jewls **erase**d them.

They forgot all about the whole thing.

Dameon had a **lousy** lunch instead of a great lunch. But five minutes later it didn't make any difference. He couldn't taste it anymore, and he was full. He went outside to play basketball and forgot about the whole thing.

Joy had a great lunch and two Tootsie Roll pops. But five minutes later it didn't make any difference. She couldn't taste it anymore, and she was full. And at **dinnertime** she was hungry, just the same.

But a **horrible** thing happened. Joy couldn't forget about **filch**ing Dameon's lunch. And for the rest of the year, every turkey sandwich, piece of chocolate cake, apple, and Tootsie Roll pop tasted like Miss Mush's porridge.

118

28. NANCY

Nancy had big hands and big feet. He didn't like his name. He thought it was a girl's name.

None of the other children in Mrs. Jewls's class thought that Nancy's name was **odd**. They didn't think of it as a girl's name or as a boy's name. Nancy was just the name of the quiet kid with the big hands and feet who sat over there in the corner next to John.

Nancy was very quiet and **shy**. He was **ashamed** of his name. He had only one friend, a girl who went to class on the twenty-third **story** of Wayside School.

They were friends for a good reason. He didn't know her name, and she didn't know his. They just called each other "Hey, you," or just **plain** "You."

Nancy was afraid to ask his friend what her name was because then he might have to tell her his name. He never could **figure out** why she never asked. But he was happy just to leave well enough alone.

One morning, Nancy and his friend were late. When they got to the twenty-third story, his friend's teacher was waiting outside.

"Hurry up. You're late, Mac," said the teacher.

Nancy's friend turned red. She didn't move.

"**Come on**, Mac, **shake a leg. Get the lead out**," said the teacher.

"Your name is Mac!" said Nancy.

Mac was very pretty. She had red hair and **freckles**. She **covered** her face and ran into the room.

"My name is Nancy!" Nancy called after her.

Mac stepped back outside. "I was ashamed to tell you my name," she said.

"Me, too," said Nancy. "Nancy's a girl's name."

"Oh, I think it's cute," said Mac.

"I like the name Mac," said Nancy.

"Mac is a boy's name," said Mac.

"My mother has a **rich aunt** named Nancy," said Nancy. "That's why she gave me the name."

"My mother once had a dog named Mac," said Mac.

120

"Hey, do you want to **trade**?" Nancy asked.

"Can we?" asked Mac.

"I don't see why not," said Nancy.

"Okay," said Mac.

They both **spun** around one hundred times in **opposite** directions until they were so **dizzy** that they fell over. When they stood up, Mac was Nancy and Nancy was Mac.

They said good-bye. Then Mac **race**d up to Mrs. Jewls's room. He was no longer shy.

"Hi, everybody. My name's Mac," he **announced**. "I traded names." He held out his big hand.

Todd jumped up and shook it. "Hi, Mac," he said. "Glad to meet you."

"How you doin', Mac," said Ron.

"**Howdy**, Mac," said Terrence.

"Nice to see you, Mac," said Bebe.

"You traded names?" asked Jason. Jason didn't like his name, either.

"That's right, Jason, old boy,[1]" said Mac.

"Is that allowed?" asked Jason.

"Why not!" said Mac.

"Hey, anybody want to trade?" Jason called.

---

1 **old boy** '어이' 또는 '친구'라는 뜻으로 주로 남자가 다른 남자를 친근하게 부를 때 쓰는 호칭이다.

"I'll trade with you," said Terrence. He didn't like his name, either.

"Wait. I'll trade with you, Terrence," said Maurecia. Maurecia didn't like her name.

"No. He's trading with me," said Jason.

"I'll trade with you, Maurecia," said Dameon.

"No, thanks," said Maurecia.

"I'll trade with you, Dameon," said Mrs. Jewls.

"No, I want to be Mrs. Jewls," said Stephen.

It **turn**ed **out** that nobody in Mrs. Jewls's class liked his name. The children all spun around in different directions until they got so dizzy that they fell over. And when they stood up again, nobody knew who anybody was.

"What are we going to do, Mrs. Jewls?" asked Leslie, who was really Eric Bacon.

"My name is not Mrs. Jewls. It's Maurecia," answered Terrence, who was really Jason.

"It is not. I'm Maurecia," said Deedee, who was really Joe.

"You're both wrong," said Maurecia. "I'm Mrs. Jewls."

This went on for an hour. At last they figured out who the real Rondi was. She was missing her two front teeth. After they figured out Rondi, they were able to get Allison pretty easily. And then from there they got D.J., Dameon, and Mrs. Jewls. She was the oldest one.

Eventually they figured out who everybody really was. They had some **difficulty** deciding which Eric was which, and actually they are still not **absolute**ly sure.

Everybody just decided to keep his own name. The children didn't like them, but it made things much easier.

Mac and Nancy kept their new names. But when they were together they still called each other "Hey, you," or just plain "You."

29. STEPHEN

Stephen had green hair. He had purple ears and a blue face. He wore his sister's pink dancing shoes and green leotards. The leotards matched his hair. He was all **dress**ed **up** as a **goblin** for Mrs. Jewls's Halloween party.

But **unfortunate**ly it wasn't Halloween.

"Ha, ha, ha, you sure look stupid," said Jason. Jason was Stephen's best friend.

"So do you," said Stephen.

"Boy, are you **dumb**," said Jenny. "Halloween is on Sunday. Today is only Friday."

"You're the one who's dumb," said Stephen. "Ha, ha, you'd probably come to school on Sunday. Mrs. Jewls said we'd have the party today."

But none of the other children wore **costume**s, only Stephen.

"All right, class," said Mrs. Jewls. "It is time for our Halloween party."

"See," said Stephen.

Mrs. Jewls gave each child a cookie that looked like an orange **witch** with a black hat. She laughed when she saw Stephen and forgot to give him one. Stephen didn't ask for it. He was afraid that she'd laugh again.

The children finished their cookies in less than thirty seconds.

"All right, class," said Mrs. Jewls. "The party is over. We have a lot of work to do."

Stephen felt like a **fool**. The party **last**ed less than a minute. And he had to **spend** the rest of the day wearing his stupid goblin **suit**.

"Look, Stephen's wearing his sister's leotards,[1]" laughed Dana.

"They're green, just like his hair," said "Fatso."

Everybody laughed.

Mrs. Jewls began the **arithmetic** lesson. She wrote on the **blackboard**. "Two plus two **equal**s five."

"That's wrong!" Joy shouted.

Mrs. Jewls tried again. "Two plus two equals three."

---

1   leotard 레오타드. 무용수나 체조 선수가 입는, 몸에 딱 붙는 옷이나 타이츠를 말한다.

That wasn't right, either. She added two and two again and got forty-three. It was **useless**. No **matter** how hard she tried, she could not get two plus two to equal four.

"I don't understand it," she said. "They've always equaled four before."

Suddenly she **scream**ed. The **chalk turned into** a **squiggling worm**! She dropped it on her foot.

Then all the lights went out, and the blackboard **lit up** like a movie **screen**.

A woman appeared on the screen. She had a long **tongue** and **pointed** ears. She stepped off the screen and into the classroom.

It was the ghost of Mrs. Gorf.

Mrs. Gorf ran her **fingernail**s across the blackboard. "**Trick** or **treat**,[2] you **rotten** kids," she said.

"Now I'll **get even with** every last one of you. Where's Todd?"

"Who is that?" asked Mrs. Jewls.

"Mrs. Gorf," said Dameon.

"Who's Mrs. Gorf?" asked Mrs. Jewls.

"She was the meanest teacher we ever had," said Rondi.

"What happened to her?" asked Mrs. Jewls.

"Louis ate her," said Jason.

"Well, I'm not going to allow this," said Mrs. Jewls. "Get out of my classroom!" she demanded.

---

2 trick or treat '과자를 안 주면 장난칠 거예요.' 핼러윈 때 아이들이 집집마다 다니며 하는 말이다.

"It's Halloween, sweet teacher," said Mrs. Gorf. "Ghosts can go anywhere they like. I've come for a little class **reunion**."

"But it isn't Halloween," said Mrs. Jewls. "Halloween is still two days away."

"I know," said Mrs. Gorf, "but Halloween **falls on** a Sunday this year, so we are **celebrating** it on the Friday before."

Stephen **leap**ed up from his seat. "See, I was right," he said. "Today is the day we celebrate it, the Friday before! Mrs. Gorf **prove**d it."

He ran up to Mrs. Gorf. "They all laughed at me and made me feel stupid because I was the only one who got dressed up. But they were the ones who were wrong. You and I are right."

He put his arms around Mrs. Gorf and hugged her.

Mrs. Gorf **gasp**ed and disappeared.

The lights came back on.

Mrs. Jewls picked up the piece of chalk from the floor. She wrote on the blackboard, "Two plus two equals four."

"That's good," she said. "When two plus two doesn't equal four, anything can happen."

All the children who had laughed at Stephen now called him a hero. But they told him to change out of his stupid costume.

So at lunch, Stephen went home, **wash**ed **up**, and changed. He came back wearing blue jeans and a polo shirt.[3] Of course, his hair was still green. It always was.

---

3   polo shirt 칼라가 달린 반소매 셔츠.

30. LOUIS

Louis had a red face and a **mustache** of many colors. He was the **yard** teacher at Wayside School. It was his job to see that the children didn't have too much fun during lunch and **recess**.

And if you haven't already guessed, he is the one who wrote this book.

On June tenth there was a **blizzard**. Louis was afraid that the children would have too much fun, so nobody was allowed outside.

"Class," said Mrs. Jewls. "After you finish your lunch today, come back up to the classroom. You are not allowed outside."

The children all went to the **lunchroom**. Miss Mush had made

Tuna Surprise.[1] They looked at it, then hurried back up the stairs.

There was nothing to do.

"Now, class," said Mrs. Jewls, "I know that you are all **bored**, but I have a special surprise for you."

"I hope it's better than the Tuna Surprise," said Maurecia.

Mrs. Jewls continued, "Louis is going to come up and **entertain** us. He will tell us a story. Now I want you all to be on your best **behavior**."

When Louis walked in, all the children **boo**ed.

"Are you going to tell us a story?" asked Bebe.

"Yes," said Louis.

"Well, it better be good," Bebe **warn**ed.

"It better be better than the Tuna Surprise," said "Butterfingers."

"I thought the Tuna Surprise was good," said Louis.

"You'd eat **dirt** if they put enough ketchup on it," said Mac.

"Hey, everybody, be quiet," said Todd. "Let him tell the story."

"Not too loud, Louis," said Sharie. "I'm trying to get some sleep."

Louis sat in the middle of the room, and all the children gathered around.

Louis began his story. "This is a story about a school very much like this one. But before we get started, there is something you **ought to** know so that you don't get **confused**. In this school

---

1 Tuna Surprise 참치를 넣어서 만든 찜 요리.

every classroom is on the same **story**."

"Which one, the eighteenth?" asked Jenny.

"No, said Louis. "They are all on the ground. The school is only one story high."

"Not much of a school," laughed Dameon.

Louis continued. "Now you might think the children there are strange and **silly**. That is probably true. However, when I told them stories about you, they thought that you were strange and silly."

"US?" the children answered. "How are we strange?"

"I'm normal," said Stephen. "Aren't I?"

"As normal as I am," Joe **assure**d him.

"The children at that school must be crazy," said Leslie.

"Real lulus,[2]" Maurecia agreed.

"Tell us about them, Louis," Bebe **demand**ed.

"For one thing," Louis said, "none of these children has ever been **turn**ed **into** an apple."

"That's silly," said Deedee. "Everybody's been turned into an apple. It's part of growing up."

Louis continued. "Dead rats don't walk into classrooms wearing **raincoat**s."

"What do they wear, **tuxedos**?" asked Todd.

"And girls never try to sell their toes," Louis added.

---

2 lulu 특이하거나 뛰어난 사람 또는 사물을 가리키는 표현. 여기서는 '괴짜' 정도로 해석할 수 있다.

"Well, **no wonder**," said Leslie, "at today's prices."

Louis continued. "They don't **trade** names or read **upside down**. They can't turn **mosquito bite**s into numbers. They don't **count** the hairs on their heads. The walls don't laugh, and two plus two always **equal**s four."

"How **horrible**," said Dameon.

"That's not the worst of it," said Louis. "They have never tasted Maurecia-**flavor**ed ice cream."

A **hush** fell over the classroom.

"Mrs. Jewls, I'm **scared**," said Allison. "Is there really a school like that?"

"Of course not," said Mrs. Jewls. "Louis was just telling a story."

"It was a good story," said Leslie.

"I thought it was stupid," said Kathy.

"I liked it," said Rondi. "It was funny."

Mrs. Jewls said, "Louis, it was a very entertaining story. But we don't really **go in for fairy tale**s here. I'm trying to teach my class the truth."

"That's all right," said Louis. "I have to go down to room twenty-nine now and tell them a story." He started out the door.

"Class," said Mrs. Jewls. "Let's all thank Louis for his wonderful story."

Everybody booed.

WORKBOOK

SIDEWAYS STORIES FROM
WAYSIDE SCHOOL

LOUIS SACHAR
ILLUSTRATED BY TIM HEITZ

Contents

'아동 도서계의 노벨상!' 미국 최고 권위의 아동 문학상

뉴베리 상(Newbery Award)은 미국 도서관 협회에서 해마다 미국 아동 문학 발전에 가장 크게 이바지한 작가에게 수여하는 아동 문학상입니다. 1922년에 시작된 이 상은 미국에서 가장 오랜 역사를 지닌 아동 문학상이자, '아동 도서계의 노벨상'이라 불릴 만큼 높은 권위를 자랑하는 상입니다.

뉴베리 상은 그 역사와 권위만큼이나 심사 기준이 까다롭기로 유명한데, 심사단은 책의 주제 의식은 물론 정보의 깊이와 스토리의 정교함, 캐릭터와 문체의 적정성 등을 꼼꼼히 평가하여 수상작을 결정합니다.

그해 최고의 작품으로 선정된 도서에게는 '뉴베리 메달(Newbery Medal)'이라고 부르는 금색 메달을 수여하며, 최종 후보에 올랐던 주목할 만한 작품들에게는 '뉴베리 아너(Newbery Honor)'라는 이름의 은색 마크를 수여합니다.

뉴베리 상을 받은 도서는 미국의 모든 도서관에 비치되어 더 많은 독자들을 만나게 되며, 대부분 수십에서 수백만 부가 판매되는 베스트셀러가 됩니다. 뉴베리 상을 수상한 작가는 그만큼 필력과 작품성을 인정받게 되어, 수상 작가의 다른 작품들 또한 수상작 못지않게 커다란 주목과 사랑을 받습니다.

왜 뉴베리 수상작인가?
쉬운 어휘로 쓰인 '검증된' 영어원서!

뉴베리 수상작들은 '검증된 원서'로 국내 영어 학습자들에게 큰 사랑을 받고 있습니다. 뉴베리 수상작이 원서 읽기에 좋은 교재인 이유는 무엇일까요?

1. 아동 문학인 만큼 어휘가 어렵지 않습니다.
2. 어렵지 않은 어휘를 사용하면서도 '문학상'을 수상한 만큼 문장의 깊이가 상당합니다.
3. 적당한 난이도의 어휘와 깊이 있는 문장으로 구성되어 있기 때문에 초등 고학년부터 성인까지, 영어 초보자부터 실력자까지 모든 영어 학습자들이 읽기에 좋습니다.

실제로 뉴베리 수상작은 국제중·특목고에서는 입시 필독서로, 대학교에서는 영어 강독 교재로 다양하고 폭넓게 활용되고 있습니다. 이런 이유로 뉴베리 수상작은 한국어 번역서보다 오히려 원서가 훨씬 많이 판매되는 기현상을 보이고 있습니다.

'베스트 오브 베스트'만을 엄선한 「뉴베리 컬렉션」

「뉴베리 컬렉션」은 뉴베리 메달 및 아너 수상작, 그리고 뉴베리 수상 작가의 유명 작품들을 엄선하여 한국 영어 학습자들을 위한 최적의 교재로 재탄생시킨 영어원서 시리즈입니다.

1. 어휘 수준과 문장의 난이도, 분량 등 국내 영어 학습자들에게 적합한 정도를 종합적으로 검토하여 선정하였습니다.
2. 기존 원서 독자층 사이의 인기도까지 감안하여 최적의 작품들을 선별하였습니다.
3. 판형이 좁고 글씨가 작아 읽기 힘들었던 원서 디자인을 대폭 수정하여, 판형을 시원하게 키우고 읽기에 최적화된 영문 서체를 사용하여 가독성을 극대화하였습니다.
4. 함께 제공되는 워크북은 어려운 어휘를 완벽하게 정리하고 이해력을 점검하는 퀴즈를 덧붙여 독자들이 원서를 보다 쉽고 재미있게 읽을 수 있도록 구성하였습니다.
5. 기존에 높은 가격에 판매되어 구입이 부담스러웠던 오디오북을 부록으로 제공하여 리스닝과 소리 내어 읽기에까지 원서를 두루 활용할 수 있도록 했습니다.

루이스 새커(Louis Sachar)는 현재 미국에서 가장 인기 있는 아동 문학 작가 중 한 사람입니다. 그는 1954년 미국 뉴욕에서 태어났으며 초등학교 보조 교사로 일한 경험을 바탕으로 쓴 『Wayside School』 시리즈로 잘 알려져 있습니다. 그 외에도 그는 『Marvin Redpost』 시리즈, 『There's a Boy in the Girls' Bathroom』, 『The Boy Who Lost His Face』 등 20여 권의 어린이책을 썼습니다. 그가 1998년에 발표한 『Holes』는 독자들의 큰 사랑을 받으며 전미도서상 등 많은 상을 수상하였고, 마침내 1999년에는 뉴베리 메달을 수상하였습니다. 2006년에는 『Holes』의 후속편 『Small Steps』를 출간하였습니다.

『Wayside School』 시리즈는 저자 루이스 새커가 학점 이수를 위해 힐사이드 초등학교(Hillside Elementary School)에서 보조 교사로 일한 경험을 바탕으로 쓴 책입니다. 그곳의 학생들은 루이스를 운동장 선생님(Louis the Yard Teacher)이라고 불렀다고 합니다. 이 시리즈의 주인공들은 힐사이드 초등학교에서 루이스가 만난 아이들의 이름에서 따왔고, 저자 자신을 반영한 인물 운동장 선생님 루이스도 등장합니다.

웨이사이드 스쿨은 원래는 1층 건물에 30개의 교실을 지을 예정이었지만, 30층 건물에 1층에 1개의 교실이 있는 건물로 지어졌습니다. 책의 주인공들은 30층에 있는 학급의 아이들 30명이고, 이들은 모두 별나고 이상합니다.

각 장마다 별나고 이상하며 때로는 초현실적인 일이 일어나는 웨이사이드 스쿨 시리즈는 미국 어린이들의 마음을 사로잡았습니다. 어린이들이 직접 선정하는 IRA-CBC Children's Choice에 선정되었고, 1,500만 부 이상의 판매를 올렸습니다. 또한 TV 애니메이션 시리즈로도 제작되어 큰 사랑을 받고 있습니다.

원서 본문

내용이 담긴 원서 본문입니다.

원어민이 읽는 일반 원서와 같은 텍스트지만, 암기해야 할 중요 어휘들은 볼드체로 표시되어 있습니다. 이 어휘들은 지금 들고 계신 워크북에 챕터별로 정리되어 있습니다.

학습 심리학 연구 결과에 따르면, 한 단어씩 따로 외우는 단어 암기는 거의 효과가 없다고 합니다. 단어를 제대로 외우기 위해서는 문맥 (context) 속에서 단어를 암기해야 하며, 한 단어당 문맥 속에서 15번 이상 마주칠 때 완벽하게 암기할 수 있다고 합니다.

이 책의 본문에서는 중요 어휘를 볼드체로 강조하여, 문맥 속의 단어들을 더 확실히 인지(word cognition in context)하도록 돕고 있습니다. 또한 대부분의 중요 단어들은 다른 챕터에서도 반복해서 등장하기 때문에 이 책을 읽는 것만으로도 자연스럽게 어휘력을 향상시킬 수 있습니다.

또한 본문 하단에는 내용 이해를 돕기 위한 '각주'가 첨가되어 있습니다. 각주는 굳이 암기할 필요는 없지만, 알아 두면 도움이 될 만한 정보를 설명하고 있습니다. 각주를 참고하면 스토리를 더 깊이 있게 이해할 수 있어 원서를 읽는 재미가 배가됩니다.

워크북(Workbook)

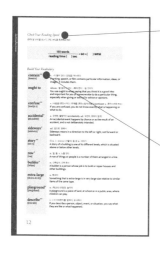

Check Your Reading Speed
해당 챕터의 단어 수가 기록되어 있어, 리딩 속도를 측정할 수 있습니다. 특히 리딩 속도를 중시하는 독자들이 유용하게 사용할 수 있습니다.

Build Your Vocabulary
본문에 볼드 표시되어 있는 단어들이 정리되어 있습니다. 리딩 전·후에 반복해서 보면 원서를 더욱 쉽게 읽을 수 있고, 어휘력도 빠르게 향상될 것입니다.

단어는 〈스펠링 – 빈도 – 발음기호 – 품사 – 한글 뜻 – 영문 뜻〉 순서로 표기되어 있으며 빈도 표시(★)가 많을수록 필수 어휘입니다. 반복해서 등장하는 단어는 빈도 대신 '복습'으로 표기되어 있습니다. 품사는 아래와 같이 표기했습니다.

n. 명사 │ a. 형용사 │ ad. 부사 │ v. 동사
conj. 접속사 │ prep. 전치사 │ int. 감탄사 │ idiom 숙어 및 관용구

Comprehension Quiz
간단한 퀴즈를 통해 읽은 내용에 대한 이해력을 점검해 볼 수 있습니다.

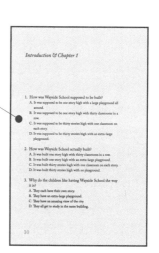

「뉴베리 컬렉션」 이렇게 읽어 보세요!

아래와 같이 프리뷰(Preview) → 리딩(Reading) → 리뷰(Review) 세 단계를 거치면서 읽으면, 더욱 효과적으로 영어 실력을 향상할 수 있습니다.

1. 프리뷰(Preview) : 오늘 읽을 내용을 먼저 점검하자!

• 워크북을 통해 오늘 읽을 챕터에 나와 있는 단어들을 쭉 훑어봅니다. 어떤 단어들이 나오는지, 내가 아는 단어와 모르는 단어는 어떤 것들이 있는지 가벼운 마음으로 살펴봅니다.

• 평소처럼 하나하나 쓰면서 암기하려고 하지는 마세요! 익숙하지 않은 단어들을 주의 깊게 보되, 어차피 리딩을 하면서 점차 익숙해질 단어라는 것을 기억하며 빠르게 훑어봅니다.

• 뒤 챕터로 갈수록 '복습'이라고 표시된 단어들이 늘어나는 것을 알 수 있습니다. '복습' 단어인데도 여전히 익숙하지 않다면 더욱 신경을 써서 봐야겠죠? 매일매일 꾸준히 읽는다면, 익숙한 단어들이 점점 많아진다는 것을 몸으로 느낄 수 있습니다.

2. 리딩(Reading) : 내용에 집중하며 빠르게 읽어 나가자!

• 프리뷰를 마친 후 바로 리딩을 시작합니다. 방금 살펴봤던 어휘들을 문장 속에서 다시 만나게 되는데, 이 과정에서 단어의 쓰임새와 어감을 자연스럽게 익히게 됩니다.

• 모르는 단어나 이해되지 않는 문장이 나오더라도 멈추지 말고 전체적인 맥락을 파악하면서 속도감 있게 읽어 나가세요. 이해되지 않는 문장들은 따로 표시를 하되, 일단 넘어가고 계속 읽는 것이 좋습니다. 뒷부분을 읽다 보면 자연히 이해가 되는 경우도 있고, 정 이해가 되지 않는 부분은 리딩을 마친 이후에 따로 리뷰하는 시간을 가지면 됩니다. 문제집을 풀듯이 모든 문장을 분석하면서 원서를 읽는 것이 아니라, 리딩을 할 때는 리딩에만, 리뷰를 할 때는 리뷰에만 집중하는 것이 필요합니다.

• 볼드 처리된 단어의 의미가 궁금하더라도 워크북을 바로 펼치지 마세요. 정 궁금하다면 한 번씩 참고하는 것도 나쁘진 않지만, 워크북과 원서를 번갈아 보면서 읽는 것은 리딩의 흐름을 끊고 단어 하나하나에 집착하는 좋지 않은 리딩 습관을 심어 줄 수 있습니다.

• 같은 맥락에서 번역서를 구해 원서와 동시에 번갈아 보는 것도 좋은 방법이 아닙니다. 한글 번역을 가지고 있다고 해도 일단 영어로 읽을 때는 영어에만 집중하고 어느 정도 분량을 읽은 후에 번역서와 비교하도록 하세요. 모든 문장을 일일이 번역해서 완벽하게 이해하려는 것은 오히려 좋지 않은 리딩 습관

을 심어 주어 장기적으로는 바람직하지 않은 결과를 얻을 수 있습니다. 처음부터 완벽하게 이해하려고 하는 것보다는 빠른 속도로 2~3회 반복해서 읽는 방식이 실력 향상에 더 도움이 됩니다. 만일 반복해서 읽어도 내용이 전혀 이해되지 않아 곤란하다면 책 선정에 문제가 있다고 할 수 있습니다. 그럴 때는 좀 더 쉬운 책을 골라 실력을 다진 뒤 다시 도전하는 것이 좋습니다.

• 초보자라면 분당 150단어의 리딩 속도를 목표로 잡고 리딩을 합니다. 분당 150단어는 원어민이 말하는 속도로, 영어 학습자들이 리스닝과 스피킹으로 넘어가기 위해 가장 기초적으로 달성해야 하는 단계입니다. 분당 50~80단어 정도의 낮은 리딩 속도를 가지고 있는 경우는 대부분 영어 실력이 부족해서라기보다 '잘못된 리딩 습관'을 가지고 있어서 그렇습니다. 이해력이 조금 떨어진다고 하더라도 분당 150단어까지는 속도에 대한 긴장감을 놓치지 말고 속도감 있게 읽어 나가도록 하세요.

3. 리뷰(Review) : 이해력을 점검하고 꼼꼼하게 다시 살펴보자!

• 해당 챕터의 Comprehension Quiz를 통해 이해력을 점검해 봅니다.

• 오늘 만난 어휘들을 다시 한번 복습합니다. 이때는 읽으면서 중요하다고 생각했던 단어를 연습장에 써 보면서 꼼꼼하게 외우는 것도 좋습니다.

• 이해가 되지 않는다고 표시해 두었던 부분도 주의 깊게 분석해 봅니다. 다시 한번 문장을 꼼꼼히 읽고, 어떤 이유에서 이해가 되지 않았는지 생각해 봅니다. 따로 메모를 남기거나 노트를 작성하는 것도 좋은 방법입니다.

• 사실 꼼꼼히 리뷰하는 것은 매우 고된 과정입니다. 원서를 읽고 리뷰하는 시간을 가지는 것이 영어 실력 향상에 많은 도움이 되기는 하지만, 이 과정을 철저히 지키려다가 원서 읽기의 재미를 반감시키는 것은 바람직하지 않습니다. 그럴 때는 차라리 리뷰를 가볍게 하는 것이 좋을 수 있습니다. '내용에 빠져서 재미있게', 문제집에서는 상상도 못할 '많은 양'을 읽으면서, 매일매일 조금씩 꾸준히 실력을 키워 가는 것이 원서를 활용하는 기본적인 방법이며, 영어 공부의 왕도입니다. 문제집 풀듯이 원서 읽기를 시도하고 접근해서는 실패할 수밖에 없습니다.

• 이런 방식으로 원서를 끝까지 다 읽었다면, 다시 반복해서 읽거나 오디오북을 활용하는 등 다양한 방식으로 원서 읽기를 확장해 나갈 수 있습니다. 이에 대한 자세한 안내가 워크북 말미에 실려 있습니다.

1. How was Wayside School supposed to be built?
   A. It was supposed to be one story high with a large playground all around.
   B. It was supposed to be one story high with thirty classrooms in a row.
   C. It was supposed to be thirty stories high with one classroom on each story.
   D. It was supposed to be thirty stories high with an extra-large playground.

2. How was Wayside School actually built?
   A. It was built one story high with thirty classrooms in a row.
   B. It was built one story high with an extra-large playground.
   C. It was built thirty stories high with one classroom on each story.
   D. It was built thirty stories high with no playground.

3. Why do the children like having Wayside School the way it is?
   A. They each have their own story.
   B. They have an extra-large playground.
   C. They have an amazing view of the city.
   D. They all get to study in the same building.

4. What did Mrs. Gorf do before turning children into apples?

   A. She wiggled her toes and blinked twice.

   B. She wiggled her ears and blinked twice.

   C. She wiggled her ears and twisted her nose.

   D. She wiggled her ears and stuck out her tongue.

5. Why did Louis think he must be wrong about Mrs. Gorf when he visited her classroom?

   A. He thought that she must be a good teacher if she ate apples.

   B. He thought that she must be a good teacher if so many children were in her class.

   C. He thought that she must be a good teacher if she taught on the thirtieth story.

   D. He thought that she must be a good teacher if so many children brought her apples.

6. How did the children stop Mrs. Gorf from turning them back into apples?

   A. They held up a mirror to turn her into an apple instead.

   B. They went to get Louis to stop Mrs. Goff.

   C. They wiggled their ears and stuck out their tongue at her.

   D. They jumped off the blackboard and bopped her on the nose.

7. How did Louis think that Mrs. Gorf would feel about him eating the apple?

   A. He thought that she would be upset since she loved apples.

   B. He thought that she would be glad that he was helping her get rid of them.

   C. He didn't think she would mind since she always had so many of them.

   D. He didn't think she would mind since she always gave them to other teachers.

Check Your Reading Speed

1분에 몇 단어를 읽는지 리딩 속도를 측정해보세요.

$$\frac{155 \text{ words}}{\text{reading time (} \quad \text{) sec}} \times 60 = (\quad) \text{ WPM}$$

Build Your Vocabulary

contain**
[kəntéin]
v. ~이 들어 있다; (감정을) 억누르다
If writing, speech, or film contains particular information, ideas, or images, it includes them.

ought to
idiom ~할 필요가 있다; ~해야 한다; ~일 것이다
You use ought to when saying that you think it is a good idea and important for you or someone else to do a particular thing, especially when giving or asking for advice or opinions.

confuse**
[kənfjúːz]
v. (사람을) 혼란시키다; (주제를) 혼란스럽게 만들다 (confused a. 혼란스러워 하는)
If you are confused, you do not know exactly what is happening or what to do.

accidental*
[æksədéntl]
a. 우연한, 돌발적인 (accidentally ad. 우연히, 뜻하지 않게)
An accidental event happens by chance or as the result of an accident, and is not deliberately intended.

sideways*
[sáidwèiz]
ad. 옆으로; 옆에서
Sideways means in a direction to the left or right, not forward or backward.

story**
[stɔ́ːri]
① n. (건물의) 층 ② n. 이야기
A story of a building is one of its different levels, which is situated above or below other levels.

row*
[rou]
n. 열, 줄; v. 노를 젓다
A row of things or people is a number of them arranged in a line.

builder*
[bíldər]
n. 건축업자, 건축 회사
A builder is a person whose job is to build or repair houses and other buildings.

extra-large
[èkstrə-láːrdʒ]
a. 특대의
Something that is extra-large is in very large size relative to similar items of the same type.

playground*
[pléigràund]
n. (학교의) 운동장; 놀이터
A playground is a piece of land, at school or in a public area, where children can play.

describe**
[diskráib]
v. (~이 어떠한지를) 말하다, 묘사하다
If you describe a person, object, event, or situation, you say what they are like or what happened.

12

silly^{**}
[síli]

a. 어리석은, 바보 같은; n. 바보
If you say that someone or something is silly, you mean that they
are foolish, childish, or ridiculous.

Check Your Reading Speed

1분에 몇 단어를 읽는지 리딩 속도를 측정해보세요.

$$\frac{922 \text{ words}}{\text{reading time ( ) sec}} \times 60 = (\quad) \text{ WPM}$$

Build Your Vocabulary

tongue**
[tʌŋ]

n. 혀; 언어; 말버릇, 말씨
Your tongue is the soft movable part inside your mouth which you use for tasting, eating, and speaking.

pointed*
[pɔ́intid]

a. (끝이) 뾰족한; (말 등이) 날카로운
Something that is pointed has a point at one end.

story^{복습}
[stɔ́:ri]

① n. (건물의) 층 ② n. 이야기
A story of a building is one of its different levels, which is situated above or below other levels.

warn***
[wɔ:rn]

v. 경고하다, 주의를 주다, 조심하라고 하다
If you warn someone not to do something, you advise them not to do it so that they can avoid possible danger or punishment.

wiggle
[wigl]

v. (좌우·상하로 짧게) 씰룩씰룩 움직이다
If you wiggle something or if it wiggles, it moves up and down or from side to side in small quick movements.

stick out

idiom ~을 내밀다, 튀어나오게 하다
If something is sticking out from a surface or object, it extends up or away from it.

turn into

idiom (~에서) ~이 되다, ~으로 변하다
To turn or be turned into something means to become that thing.

count***
[kaunt]

v. 수를 세다; 계산에 넣다; 중요하다; n. 셈, 계산
When you count, you say all the numbers one after another up to a particular number.

cheat**
[tʃi:t]

v. (시험·경기 등에서) 부정행위를 하다; 속이다, 사기 치다
When someone cheats, they do not obey a set of rules which they should be obeying, for example in a game or exam.

opinion**
[əpínjən]

n. 의견, 견해, 생각
Your opinion about something is what you think or believe about it.

scare**
[skɛər]

v. 겁주다, 놀라게 하다 (scared a. 무서워하는, 겁먹은)
If you are scared of someone or something, you are frightened of them.

absolute*
[ǽbsəlù:t]

a. 완전한, 완벽한; 확실한 (absolutely ad. 극도로, 굉장히; 틀림없이)
Absolutely means totally and completely.

sneeze*
[sni:z]

v. 재채기하다; n. 재채기
When you sneeze, you suddenly take in your breath and then blow it down your nose noisily without being able to stop yourself, for example because you have a cold.

bless*
[bles]

v. (신의) 축복을 빌다
You can say 'bless you' to someone who has just sneezed.

run away

idiom (~에서) 달아나다
If you run away, you move quickly away from someone or a place or escape from them or there.

halfway*
[hǽfwèi]

ad. (거리·시간상으로) 중간, 가운데쯤에
Halfway means in the middle of a place or between two points, at an equal distance from each of them.

chalk**
[tʃɔ:k]

n. 분필
A chalk is a small piece of soft white rock, used for writing or drawing with.

dozen**
[dʌzn]

n. 12개짜리 묶음, 다스; 다수, 여러 개
If you have a dozen things, you have twelve of them.

yard**
[ja:rd]

n. (학교의) 운동장; 마당, 뜰; 정원
A yard is a flat area of concrete or stone that is next to a building and often has a wall around it.

recess*
[risés]

n. (학교의) 쉬는 시간; (의회·위원회 등의) 휴회 기간
A recess is a break between classes at a school.

investigate*
[invéstəgèit]

v. 조사하다, 살피다; 연구하다
If someone, especially an official, investigates an event, situation, or claim, they try to find out what happened or what is the truth.

playground^{복습}
[pléigràund]

n. (학교의) 운동장; 놀이터
A playground is a piece of land, at school or in a public area, where children can play.

flight of stairs

idiom 한 줄로 이어진 계단
A flight of stairs is a set of steps or stairs that lead from one level to another without changing direction.

bop
[bap]

v. (가볍게) 때리다; n. 비밥(재즈의 일종)
If you bop something, you hit it lightly, not hard.

demand***
[dimǽnd]

v. 요구하다; 강력히 묻다, 따지다; n. 요구 (사항); 수요
If you demand something such as information or action, you ask for it in a very forceful way.

scream*
[skri:m]

v. 비명을 지르다, 괴성을 지르다; n. 비명, 절규
When someone screams, they make a very loud, high-pitched cry, because they are in pain or are very frightened.

after all

idiom 어쨌든; (예상과는 달리) 결국에는
You use after all when introducing a statement which supports or helps explain something you have just said.

1. Why were the children on the thirtieth floor afraid of Mrs. Jewls?
   A. They had heard that she would be nice, and they never had a nice teacher.
   B. They had heard that she would be nice, and they used to have a nice teacher.
   C. They had heard that she would be mean, and they never had a mean teacher.
   D. They had heard that she would be mean, and they used to have a mean teacher.

2. Why did Mrs. Jewls think that she was teaching a class full of monkeys?
   A. She thought that they all looked hairy.
   B. She thought that they sounded like monkeys.
   C. She thought that they were too cute to be children.
   D. She thought that they all liked eating bananas too much.

3. How did Todd feel about not being thought of as a monkey anymore?
   A. He thought that he wouldn't go to the zoo.
   B. He thought that he wouldn't get a banana.
   C. He thought that he would have to take a bath.
   D. He thought that he would have to do more homework.

4. Why did Joe not go to recess?

    A. Joe had broken his leg.

    B. Joe was being disciplined.

    C. Joe had to learn how to spell.

    D. Joe had to learn how to count.

5. How did Joe feel about his way of counting?

    A. He thought that nobody cared about how he counted.

    B. He thought that when he counted his way he got the wrong answer.

    C. He thought that when he counted right he got the wrong answer.

    D. He thought that learning to count the right way was important.

6. What did Mrs. Jewls say that school was good for?

    A. Speeding up learning

    B. Making new friends

    C. Sleeping in class

    D. Playing at recess

7. What happened when Joe woke up the next day?

    A. He knew how to read.

    B. He knew how to count.

    C. He knew how to spell.

    D. He knew how to add.

Check Your Reading Speed

1분에 몇 단어를 읽는지 리딩 속도를 측정해보세요.

$$\frac{684 \text{ words}}{\text{reading time ( ) sec}} \times 60 = (\quad) \text{ WPM}$$

Build Your Vocabulary

terrible*
[térəbl]

a. 극심한, 엄청난; 끔찍한, 소름 끼치는; 형편없는
(terribly ad. 몹시, 극심하게)
You use terrible to emphasize the great extent or degree of
something.

scare복습
[skɛər]

v. 겁주다, 놀라게 하다 (scared a. 무서워하는, 겁먹은)
If you are scared of someone or something, you are frightened
of them.

wind
[waind]

① v. (도로·강 등이) 구불구불하다; 감다 (winding a. 구불구불한) ② n. 바람
If a road, river, or line of people winds in a particular direction,
it goes in that direction with a lot of bends or twists in it.

creak
[kriːk]

v. 삐걱거리다; n. 삐걱거리는 소리
If something creaks, it makes a short, high-pitched sound when
it moves.

staircase*
[stéərkèis]

n. (건물 내부에 난간으로 죽 이어져 있는) 계단
A staircase is a set of stairs inside a building.

horrible
[hɔ́ːrəbl]

a. 지긋지긋한, 끔찍한; 소름 끼치는, 무시무시한 (horribly ad. 몹시)
Horrible is used to emphasize how bad something is.

ridiculous
[ridíkjuləs]

a. 웃기는, 말도 안 되는, 터무니없는
If you say that something or someone is ridiculous, you mean
that they are very foolish.

all the way

idiom 내내, 시종; 완전히
You use all the way to emphasize how long a distance is.

flight of stairs복습

idiom 한 줄로 이어진 계단
A flight of stairs is a set of steps or stairs that lead from one
level to another without changing direction.

zookeeper
[zúːkìːpər]

n. 동물원 사육사
A zookeeper is a person who works in a zoo, taking care of the
animals.

scratch*
[skrætʃ]

v. (가려운 데를) 긁다; 긁힌 자국을 내다; n. 긁힌 자국
If you scratch yourself, you rub your fingernails against your
skin because it is itching.

get wrong

idiom ~의 말을 오해하다
If you get someone wrong, you do not understand correctly
what they mean.

expect***
[ikspékt]

v. 예상하다, 기대하다
If you expect something to happen, you believe that it will happen.

flabbergasted
[flǽbərgæstid]

a. 크게 놀란
If you say that you are flabbergasted, you are emphasizing that you are extremely surprised.

purse*
[pəːrs]

n. 핸드백; (여성용의 작은) 지갑
A purse is a small bag that women carry.

subtract*
[səbtrǽkt]

v. (수·양을) 빼다 (subtraction n. 뺄셈)
If you subtract one number from another, you do a calculation in which you take it away from the other number. For example, if you subtract 3 from 5, you get 2.

spell**
[spel]

v. 철자를 맞게 쓰다, 맞춤법에 맞게 글을 쓰다; (어떤 단어의) 철자를 말하다
(spelling n. 철자법, 맞춤법)
When you spell a word, you write or speak each letter in the word in the correct order.

tap*
[tæp]

v. (가볍게) 톡톡 두드리다; 박자를 맞추다; n. 수도꼭지; (가볍게) 두드리기
If you tap something, you hit it with a quick light blow or a series of quick light blows.

blackboard*
[blǽkbɔ̀ːrd]

n. 칠판
A blackboard is a dark-colored board that you can write on with chalk.

discipline**
[dísəplin]

n. 규율, 훈육; 단련법, 수련법
Discipline is the practice of making people obey rules or standards of behavior, and punishing them when they do not.

Check Your Reading Speed

1분에 몇 단어를 읽는지 리딩 속도를 측정해보세요.

$$\frac{858 \text{ words}}{\text{reading time ( ) sec}} \times 60 = (\quad) \text{ WPM}$$

Build Your Vocabulary

curly[*]
[kə́ːrli]

a. 곱슬곱슬한
If you have curly hair, it means that your hair is made, growing, or arranged in a round or curved shapes.

count^{복습}
[kaunt]

v. 수를 세다; 계산에 넣다; 중요하다; n. 셈, 계산
When you count, you say all the numbers one after another up to a particular number.

recess^{복습}
[risés]

n. (학교의) 쉬는 시간; (의회·위원회 등의) 휴회 기간
A recess is a break between classes at a school.

shrug[*]
[ʃrʌg]

v. (어깨를) 으쓱하다
If you shrug, you raise your shoulders to show that you are not interested in something or that you do not know or care about something.

cover[***]
[kʌ́vər]

v. 덮다; (감추거나 보호하기 위해) 씌우다, 가리다; 다루다, 포함시키다; n. 덮개
If one thing covers another, it forms a layer over its surface.

prove[**]
[pruːv]

v. 입증하다, 증명하다; (~임이) 드러나다
If you prove that something is true, you show by means of argument or evidence that it is definitely true.

correct[***]
[kərékt]

a. 맞는, 정확한; 적절한, 옳은; v. 바로잡다, 정정하다
If something is correct, it is in accordance with the facts and has no mistakes.

erase[*]
[iréis]

v. (지우개 등으로) 지우다; (완전히) 없애다 (eraser n. 고무 지우개)
An eraser is an object, usually a piece of rubber or plastic, which is used for removing something that has been written using a pencil or a pen.

make sense

idiom 이해가 되다; 타당하다; 이해하기 쉽다
If something makes sense, you can understand it.

kickball
[kíkbɔːl]

n. 발야구
Kickball is an informal game combining elements of baseball and soccer, in which a soccer ball is thrown to a person who kicks it and proceeds to run the bases.

beat[**]
[biːt]

v. (아주 세게 계속) 때리다; (게임·시합에서) 이기다; n. 고동, 맥박; 리듬
If you beat someone or something, you hit them very hard.

blackboard^{복습}
[blǽkbɔ̀ːrd]

n. 칠판
A blackboard is a dark-colored board that you can write on with chalk.

discipline^{복습}
[dísəplin]

n. 규율, 훈육; 단련법, 수련법
Discipline is the practice of making people obey rules or standards of behavior, and punishing them when they do not.

get it

idiom 알다, 이해하다
You can say get it when you understand something or get the right answer.

speed***
[spiːd]

v. 더 빠르게 하다, 가속화하다; 빨리 가다; n. (물체의 이동) 속도
If you speed something, you make it happen more quickly.

exact***
[igzǽkt]

a. 정확한, 정밀한; 꼼꼼한, 빈틈없는 (exactly ad. 맞아; 정확히, 꼭)
If you say 'Exactly,' you are agreeing with someone or emphasizing the truth of what they say.

1. What did Sharie always wear to school?
   A. She always wore a big yellow raincoat with a hood.
   B. She always wore a big yellow sweatshirt with a hood.
   C. She always wore a big red and blue raincoat with a hood.
   D. She always wore a big red and blue overcoat with a hood.

2. How did Mrs. Jewls feel about Sharie looking out the window or sleeping in class?
   A. Mrs. Jewls thought that Sharie did her best learning when she did those things.
   B. Mrs. Jewls thought that Sharie never learned anything in her class.
   C. Mrs. Jewls thought that Sharie needed a break from studying so hard.
   D. Mrs. Jewls thought that Sharie was distracted and needed discipline.

3. How did Sharie react when she feel out the window?
   A. She woke up and thought that she was dreaming.
   B. She woke up, was confused, and then went back to sleep.
   C. She slept until she landed safely on the ground.
   D. She woke up and screamed for help.

4. Why did Mrs. Jewls write Todd's name under DISCIPLINE?

    A. Todd answered a question wrong.

    B. Todd hit another student.

    C. Todd had screamed in class.

    D. Todd spoke in class.

5. Which of the following was NOT one of the three chances Mrs. Jewls gave children in her class?

    A. Writing the student's name on the blackboard

    B. Circling the student's name on the blackboard

    C. Making the student stand in the corner near the blackboard

    D. Putting a check next to the student's name on the blackboard

6. What happened to Todd every day ever since Mrs. Jewls took over class?

    A. Todd always got sick and had to go home early.

    B. Todd always needed discipline and had to go home early.

    C. Todd always forgot to bring his lunch and had to go home early.

    D. Todd always forgot to bring his homework and had to go home early.

7. Why did Joy have to start her workbook all the way at the beginning?

    A. Todd had given her workbook to robbers.

    B. Todd had let Joy cheat from his workbook.

    C. Joy had finished her workbook the wrong way.

    D. Joy had left her workbook at home.

Check Your Reading Speed

1분에 몇 단어를 읽는지 리딩 속도를 측정해보세요.

$$\frac{544 \text{ words}}{\text{reading time ( ) sec}} \times 60 = (\quad) \text{ WPM}$$

Build Your Vocabulary

eyelash
[áilæ̀ʃ]

n. 속눈썹
Your eyelashes are the hairs which grow on the edges of your eyelids.

weigh**
[wei]

v. 무게가 ~이다; 무게를 달다
If someone or something weighs a particular amount, this amount is how heavy they are.

overcoat*
[óuvərkòut]

n. 외투, 오버코트
An overcoat is a thick warm coat that you wear in winter.

hood*
[hud]

n. (외투 등에 달린) 모자; 복면
A hood is a part of a coat which you can pull up to cover your head.

spend***
[spend]

v. (spent-spent) (시간을) 보내다; (돈을) 쓰다
If you spend time or energy doing something, you use your time or effort doing it.

stare*
[stɛər]

v. 빤히 쳐다보다, 응시하다; n. 빤히 쳐다보기, 응시
If you stare at someone or something, you look at them for a long time.

fall asleep

idiom 잠들다
When you fall asleep, you start sleeping.

arithmetic*
[əríθmətik]

n. 산수, 연산; 산술, 계산
Arithmetic is the part of mathematics that is concerned with the addition, subtraction, multiplication, and division of numbers.

bury**
[béri]

v. (보이지 않게) 묻다; (시신을) 묻다, 매장하다
If you bury your head or face in something, you press your head or face against it.

snore*
[snɔːr]

v. 코를 골다; n. 코 고는 소리
When someone who is asleep snores, they make a loud noise each time they breathe.

awful**
[ɔ́ːfəl]

a. (양적으로 많음을 강조하는 의미로) 엄청; 끔찍한, 지독한
You can use awful with noun groups that refer to an amount in order to emphasize how large that amount is.

toss and turn

idiom (자면서) 계속 몸을 뒤치락거리다
If you toss and turn, you keep moving around in bed and cannot sleep properly, for example because you are ill or worried.

flop
[flap]

v. 털썩 주저앉다, 드러눕다; (무겁게) 매달리다; 완전히 실패하다; n. 실패작
If you flop into a chair or a bed, for example, you sit or lie down heavily and suddenly, especially when very tired.

roll**
[roul]

v. 구르다, 굴러가다; 굴리다; 돌(리)다; n. 통, 두루마리
When something rolls or when you roll it, it moves along a surface, turning over many times.

scream^{복습}
[skri:m]

v. 비명을 지르다, 괴성을 지르다; n. 비명, 절규
When someone screams, they make a very loud, high-pitched cry, because they are in pain or are very frightened.

sound asleep

idiom 깊이 잠들다
If someone is sound asleep, they are sleeping very deeply.

confuse^{복습}
[kənfjú:z]

v. (사람을) 혼란시키다; (주제를) 혼란스럽게 만들다
(confused a. 혼란스러워 하는)
If you are confused, you do not know exactly what is happening or what to do.

figure out

idiom (생각한 끝에) ~을 이해하다; (양·비용을) 계산하다
If you figure out someone or something, you come to understand them by thinking carefully.

yawn[*]
[jɔ:n]

v. 하품하다; n. 하품
If you yawn, you open your mouth very wide and breathe in more air than usual, often when you are tired or when you are not interested in something.

exceptional[*]
[iksépʃənl]

a. 이례적일 정도로 우수한, 특출한 (exceptionally ad. 유난히, 특별히)
You use exceptional to describe someone or something that has a particular quality, usually a good quality, to an unusually high degree.

yard^{복습}
[ja:rd]

n. (학교의) 운동장; 마당, 뜰; 정원
A yard is a flat area of concrete or stone that is next to a building and often has a wall around it.

way^{***}
[wei]

ad. 아주 멀리; 큰 차이로, 훨씬; n. 방법, 방식; (어떤 곳에 이르는) 길
You can use way to emphasize, for example, that something is a great distance away or is very much below or above a particular level or amount.

duck^{**}
[dʌk]

v. (머리나 몸을) 휙 수그리다; (머리나 몸을 움직여) 피하다; n. 오리
If you duck, you move your head or the top half of your body quickly downward to avoid something that might hit you, or to avoid being seen.

volleyball[*]
[válibɔ̀:l]

n. 배구
Volleyball is a game in which two teams hit a large ball with their hands backwards and forwards over a high net.

net^{**}
[net]

n. (스포츠에서 공이 넘어 다니는) 네트; 망사, 레이스; 그물
In games such as tennis, the net is the piece of netting across the center of the court which the ball has to go over.

hurtle
[hə:rtl]

v. 돌진하다
If someone or something hurtles somewhere, they move there very quickly, often in a rough or violent way.

kickball^{복습}
[kíkbɔːl]

n. 발야구
Kickball is an informal game combining elements of baseball and soccer, in which a soccer ball is thrown to a person who kicks it and proceeds to run the bases.

field***
[fiːld]

n. 경기장; 들판, 밭; (도서관·실험실 등이 아닌) 현장; v. 수비를 보다
A sports field is an area of grass where sports are played.

hop*
[hap]

v. 깡충깡충 뛰다; 급히 가다; n. 깡충 뛰기
If you hop, you move along by jumping on one foot.

court**
[kɔːrt]

n. (테니스 등을 하는) 코트; 법정, 법원
A court is an area in which you play a game such as tennis, basketball, badminton, or squash.

speed^{복습}
[spiːd]

v. (sped/speeded-sped/speeded) 빨리 가다; 더 빠르게 하다, 가속화하다; n. (물체의 이동) 속도
If you speed somewhere, you move or travel there quickly, usually in a vehicle.

cheer**
[tʃiər]

v. 환호성을 지르다, 환호하다; n. 환호(성), 응원의 함성
When people cheer, they shout loudly to show their approval or to encourage someone who is doing something such as taking part in a game.

bother*
[báðər]

v. 귀찮게 하다, 귀찮게 말을 걸다; 신경 쓰다, 애를 쓰다; n. 성가심
If someone bothers you, they talk to you when you want to be left alone or interrupt you when you are busy.

stand***
[stænd]

v. 참다, 견디다; 서다, 서 있다; 상대하다; n. 태도, 의견
If you cannot stand something, you cannot bear it or tolerate it.

Check Your Reading Speed

1분에 몇 단어를 읽는지 리딩 속도를 측정해보세요.

$$\frac{813 \text{ words}}{\text{reading time ( ) sec}} \times 60 = (\ ) \text{ WPM}$$

Build Your Vocabulary

carry on	idiom 투덜대다 If someone carry on, they behave in an excited or anxious way that is not controlled.
light up	idiom (얼굴이) 환해지다; 빛나게 만들다 If someone's eyes or face light up, or something lights them up, they become bright with excitement or happiness.
know better	idiom (~할 정도로) 어리석지는 않다 If someone knows better than to do something, they are old enough or experienced enough to know it is the wrong thing to do.
amaze[*] [əméiz]	v. (대단히) 놀라게 하다 (amazement n. (대단한) 놀라움) Amazement is the feeling you have when something surprises you very much.
workbook [wɔ́:rkbùk]	n. 연습 문제집 A workbook is a book to help you learn a particular subject which has questions in it with spaces for the answers.
scratch[복습] [skrǽtʃ]	v. (가려운 데를) 긁다; 긁힌 자국을 내다; n. 긁힌 자국 If you scratch yourself, you rub your fingernails against your skin because it is itching.
tap[복습] [tǽp]	v. (가볍게) 톡톡 두드리다; 박자를 맞추다; n. 수도꼭지; (가볍게) 두드리기 If you tap something, you hit it with a quick light blow or a series of quick light blows.
whisper[*] [hwíspər]	v. 속삭이다, 소곤거리다, 귓속말을 하다; n. 속삭임, 소곤거리는 소리 When you whisper, you say something very quietly.
ignore[**] [ignɔ́:r]	v. (사람을) 못 본 척하다, 무시하다 If you ignore someone or something, you pay no attention to them.
poke[*] [pouk]	v. (손가락 등으로) 쿡 찌르다; 쑥 내밀다; n. 찌르기, 쑤시기 If you poke someone or something, you quickly push them with your finger or with a sharp object.
pretend[***] [priténd]	v. ~인 척하다, ~인 것처럼 굴다; ~라고 가장하다 If you pretend that something is the case, you act in a way that is intended to make people believe that it is the case, although in fact it is not.
notice[***] [nóutis]	v. ~을 의식하다; 주목하다, 관심을 기울이다; n. 신경 씀, 알아챔; 공고문 If you notice something or someone, you become aware of them.

sharpen*
[ʃáːrpən]

v. 날카롭게 하다, (날카롭게) 깎다; (느낌·감정이) 더 강렬해지다
If you sharpen an object, you make its edge very thin or you make its end pointed.

dumb*
[dʌm]

a. 멍청한, 바보 같은; 벙어리의, 말을 못 하는
If you call a person dumb, you mean that they are stupid or foolish.

race
[reis]

n. 경쟁; 경주, 달리기 (시합); 인종, 종족; v. 경주하다, 경쟁하다; 급히 가다
A race is a competition to see who is the fastest, for example in running, swimming, or driving.

demand^{복습}
[diménd]

v. 강력히 묻다, 따지다; 요구하다; n. 요구 (사항); 수요
If you demand something such as information or action, you ask for it in a very forceful way.

bother^{복습}
[báðər]

v. 귀찮게 하다, 귀찮게 말을 걸다; 신경 쓰다, 애를 쓰다; n. 성가심
If someone bothers you, they talk to you when you want to be left alone or interrupt you when you are busy.

kindergarten
[kíndərgàːrtn]

n. 유치원
A kindergarten is an informal kind of school for very young children, where they learn things by playing.

take over

idiom (~로부터) (~을) 인계받다, (기업 등을) 인수하다
If you take over something from someone, you do it instead of them.

strike***
[straik]

n. (야구에서) 스트라이크; 파업; 치기; v. (세게) 치다, 부딪치다; (갑자기) 공격하다
In baseball, a strike is a pitched ball judged good but missed or not swung at, three of which cause a batter to be out.

seal*
[siːl]

v. (봉투 등을) 봉인하다; 밀봉하다; n. 직인
If you seal a container or an opening, you cover it with something in order to prevent air, liquid, or other material getting in or out.

knock**
[nak]

n. 문 두드리는 소리;
v. (문 등을) 두드리다; (때리거나 타격을 가해) ~한 상태가 되게 만들다
A knock is the sound of someone hitting a door or window, with their hand or with something hard to attract attention.

nickel*
[níkəl]

n. (미국·캐나다의) 5센트(짜리 동전); (금속 원소) 니켈
In the United States and Canada, a nickel is a coin worth five cents.

dime*
[daim]

n. (미국·캐나다의) 10센트(짜리 동전)
A dime is an American coin worth ten cents.

robber*
[rábər]

n. 강도
A robber is someone who steals money or property from a bank, a shop, or a vehicle, often by using force or threats.

all the way^{복습}

idiom 내내, 시종; 완전히
You use all the way to emphasize how long a distance is.

valuable**
[vǽljuəbl]

a. 가치가 큰, 값비싼; 소중한, 귀중한
Valuable objects are objects which are worth a lot of money.

knowledge**
[nálidʒ]

n. 지식; (특정 사실·상황에 대해) 알고 있음
Knowledge is information and understanding about a subject which a person has, or which all people have.

grab*
[græb]

v. (와락·단단히) 붙잡다; ~을 잡으려고 하다; n. 와락 잡아채려고 함
If you grab something, you take it or pick it up suddenly and roughly.

give up

idiom 포기하다, 그만두다, 단념하다
If you give up, you decide that you cannot do something and stop trying to do it.

criminal**
[krímənl]

n. 범인, 범죄자; a. 범죄의; 형사상의
A criminal is a person who regularly commits crimes.

complain**
[kəmpléin]

v. 불평하다, 항의하다
If you complain about a situation, you say that you are not satisfied with it.

sigh*
[sai]

v. 한숨을 쉬다, 한숨짓다; n. 한숨
When you sigh, you let out a deep breath, as a way of expressing feelings such as disappointment, tiredness, or pleasure.

triumphant
[traiÁmfənt]

a. 의기양양한; 큰 승리를 거둔 (triumphantly ad. 의기양양하여)
Someone who is triumphant has gained a victory or succeeded in something and feels very happy about it.

field^{복습}
[fi:ld]

n. 경기장; 들판, 밭; (도서관·실험실 등이 아닌) 현장; v. 수비를 보다
A sports field is an area of grass where sports are played.

clap*
[klæp]

v. 박수를 치다, 손뼉을 치다; n. 박수 (소리)
When you clap, you hit your hands together to show appreciation or attract attention.

whistle**
[hwisl]

v. 휘파람을 불다, 휘파람 소리를 내다; 호루라기를 불다; n. 호루라기; 휘파람 (소리)
When you whistle or when you whistle a tune, you make a series of musical notes by forcing your breath out between your lips, or your teeth.

Chapters 6 & 7

1. What could Bebe do faster than anyone else in her class?
   A. She could count faster than anyone else.
   B. She could spell faster than anyone else.
   C. She could draw faster than anyone else.
   D. She could talk faster than anyone else.

2. Why did Calvin assist Bebe during art class?
   A. Calvin hated art.
   B. Calvin wanted Bebe to be his friend.
   C. Calvin was a great artist and gave Bebe advice.
   D. Calvin didn't think he was good at art.

3. How did Mrs. Jewls say that art was measured?
   A. She said it was measured by how good the pictures were.
   B. She said it was measured by how many pieces you produce.
   C. She said it was measured by how many pieces you give to friends.
   D. She said it was measured by how much time was spent on one picture.

4. What did Mrs. Jewls want Calvin to do?
   A. She wanted him to help Bebe with her art.
   B. She wanted him to deliver a note to Miss Zarves.
   C. She wanted him to deliver a message to Louis.
   D. She wanted him to go to recess early.

5. Which of the following was NOT true about Calvin's task and Wayside School?

   A. There was no Miss Zarves.

   B. There was no nineteenth floor.

   C. There was no note from Mrs. Jewls.

   D. There were no stairs in Wayside School.

6. How did Mrs. Jewls first react to Calvin when he returned to class?

   A. She asked him how Miss Zarves was doing.

   B. She asked him how he got to the nineteenth story.

   C. She thanked him and was glad she could count on him.

   D. She thanked him for pretending to go to the nineteenth story.

7. Why did Mrs. Jewls say that the note was important?

   A. The note asked Miss Zarves not to meet her for lunch.

   B. The note asked Miss Zarves for advice for a lesson.

   C. The note asked Miss Zarves to switch classrooms with her.

   D. The note asked Miss Zarves to come watch a movie with her class.

Check Your Reading Speed

1분에 몇 단어를 읽는지 리딩 속도를 측정해보세요.

$$\frac{704 \text{ words}}{\text{reading time ( ) sec}} \times 60 = (\text{) WPM}$$

Build Your Vocabulary

period**
[píːəriəd]

n. (학교의 일과를 나눠 놓은) 시간; 기간, 시기; 마침표
At a school or college, a period is one of the parts that the day is divided into during which lessons or other activities take place.

assistant*
[əsístənt]

n. 조수, 보조원; a. 보좌의, 보조의
Someone's assistant is a person who helps them in their work.

masterpiece*
[mǽstərpìːs]

n. 걸작, 명작
A masterpiece is an extremely good painting, novel, film, or other work of art.

sheet**
[ʃiːt]

n. (종이) 한 장; 침대에 깔거나 위로 덮는 얇은 천
A sheet of paper is a rectangular piece of paper.

crayon
[kréian]

n. 크레용
A crayon is a pencil containing colored wax or clay, or a rod of colored wax used for drawing.

run low

idiom (자금 따위가) 고갈되다, 모자라게 되다
If a supply of something is running low, there is not much of it left.

waste**
[weist]

v. (돈·시간 등을) 낭비하다; 헛되이 쓰다; n. 쓰레기, 폐기물; 낭비
If you waste something such as time, money, or energy, you use too much of it doing something that is not important or necessary, or is unlikely to succeed.

stack*
[stæk]

n. 무더기, 더미; v. (깔끔하게 정돈하여) 쌓다
A stack of things is a pile of them.

hardly***
[háːrdli]

ad. ~하자마자; 거의 ~아니다; 거의 ~할 수가 없다
If you say hardly had one thing happened when something else happened, you mean that the first event was followed immediately by the second.

leaf**
[liːf]

n. (나뭇)잎; (책의) 낱장
The leaves of a tree or plant are the parts that are flat, thin, and usually green.

hand***
[hænd]

v. 건네주다, 넘겨주다; n. 손
If you hand something to someone, you pass it to them.

remarkable*
[rimáːrkəbl]

a. 놀랄 만한, 놀라운, 주목할 만한
Someone or something that is remarkable is unusual or special in a way that makes people notice them and be surprised or impressed.

announce[star][star]
[ənáuns]

v. 발표하다, 알리다; (공공장소에서) 방송으로 알리다
If you announce something, you tell people about it publicly or officially.

sigh[복습]
[sai]

v. 한숨을 쉬다, 한숨짓다; n. 한숨
When you sigh, you let out a deep breath, as a way of expressing feelings such as disappointment, tiredness, or pleasure.

lean[star][star]
[li:n]

v. ~에 기대다; 기울다, (몸을) 숙이다; a. 군살이 없는, 호리호리한
If you lean on or against someone or something, you rest against them so that they partly support your weight.

break a record

idiom 기록을 경신하다
If you break a record, you beat the previous record for a particular achievement.

pile[star][star]
[pail]

n. 포개 놓은 것, 더미; v. (물건을 차곡차곡) 쌓다
A pile of things is a quantity of things that have been put neatly somewhere so that each thing is on top of the one below.

shake hands

idiom 악수하다
If you shake hands with someone, you take their right hand in your own for a few moments, often moving it up and down slightly.

measure[star][star]
[méʒər]

v. (중요성·가치·영향을) 판단하다; (치수·양 등을) 측정하다; n. 조치
If you measure the quality, value, or effect of something, you discover or judge how great it is.

spend[복습]
[spend]

v. (시간을) 보내다; (돈을) 쓰다
If you spend time or energy doing something, you use your time or effort doing it.

garbage[star]
[gáːrbidʒ]

n. 쓰레기(통)
A garbage is a container where people put things that are being thrown away.

pail[star]
[peil]

n. 들통, 버킷 (garbage pail n. 쓰레기통)
A pail is a bucket, usually made of metal or wood.

crumple
[krʌmpl]

v. 구기다; 구겨지다; (얼굴이) 일그러지다; 쓰러지다
If you crumple something such as paper or cloth, or if it crumples, it is squashed and becomes full of untidy creases and folds.

playground[복습]
[pléigràund]

n. (학교의) 운동장; 놀이터
A playground is a piece of land, at school or in a public area, where children can play.

spot[star][star]
[spat]

v. 발견하다, 찾다, 알아채다; n. (작은) 점, 반점
If you spot something or someone, you notice them.

doubt[star][star][star]
[daut]

v. 확신하지 못하다, 의심하다, 의문을 갖다; n. 의심, 의혹, 의문
If you doubt whether something is true or possible, you believe that it is probably not true or possible.

whisker[star]
[wískər]

n. (고양이·쥐 등의) 수염; 구레나룻
The whiskers of an animal such as a cat or a mouse are the long stiff hairs that grow near its mouth.

Check Your Reading Speed

1분에 몇 단어를 읽는지 리딩 속도를 측정해보세요.

$$\frac{755 \text{ words}}{\text{reading time ( ) sec}} \times 60 = (\quad) \text{ WPM}$$

Build Your Vocabulary

story ^{복습}
[stɔ́ːri]

① n. (건물의) 층 ② n. 이야기
A story of a building is one of its different levels, which is situated above or below other levels.

establish***
[estǽbliʃ]

v. (사실을) 규명하다; 설립하다, 설정하다
If you establish that something is true, you discover facts that show that it is definitely true.

patience*
[péiʃəns]

n. 참을성; 인내력, 인내심
If you have patience, you are able to stay calm and not get annoyed, for example when something takes a long time, or when someone is not doing what you want them to do.

kindergarten ^{복습}
[kíndərgàːrtn]

n. 유치원
A kindergarten is an informal kind of school for very young children, where they learn things by playing.

hoot
[huːt]

v. 폭소를 터뜨리다; 콧방귀를 뀌다, 비웃다; (자동차 경적을) 빵빵거리다
If you hoot, you make a loud high-pitched noise when you are laughing or showing disapproval.

builder ^{복습}
[bíldər]

n. 건축업자, 건축 회사
A builder is a person whose job is to build or repair houses and other buildings.

accidental ^{복습}
[æksədéntl]

a. 우연한, 돌발적인 (accidentally ad. 우연히, 뜻하지 않게)
An accidental event happens by chance or as the result of an accident, and is not deliberately intended.

sideways ^{복습}
[sáidwèiz]

ad. 옆으로; 옆에서
Sideways means in a direction to the left or right, not forward or backward.

besides**
[bisáidz]

ad. 게다가, 뿐만 아니라; prep. ~외에
Besides is used to emphasize an additional point that you are making, especially one that you consider to be important.

administration**
[ədmìnistréiʃən]

n. 관리, 행정; 집행 (administration office n. 행정실)
The administration of a company or institution is the group of people who organize and supervise it.

mailbox*
[méilbàks]

n. (개인의) 우편함; 우체통
A mailbox is a box outside your house where your letters are delivered.

34

shoot***
[ʃuːt]

v. 슛을 하다; (총 등을) 쏘다; 휙 움직이다; n. 촬영
In sports such as football or basketball, when someone shoots, they try to score by kicking, throwing, or hitting the ball toward the goal.

basket**
[bǽskit]

n. (농구에서) 바스켓; 바구니
In basketball, the basket is a net hanging from a ring through which players try to throw the ball in order to score points.

toss*
[tɔːs]

v. (가볍게·아무렇게나) 던지다; n. (고개를) 홱 젖히기
If you toss something somewhere, you throw it there lightly, often in a rather careless way.

dribble
[dribl]

v. 드리블하다; 질질 흘리다; n. (액체가) 조금씩 흘러내리는 것
When players dribble the ball in a game such as football or basketball, they keep kicking or tapping it quickly in order to keep it moving.

take a shot

idiom (농구·축구에서) 슛을 하다; 시도하다
If you take a shot, you attempt to score a point by throwing, hitting, or kicking a ball.

tip*
[tip]

v. (어떤 것이 어느 방향으로 가도록) 살짝 건드리다; 기울어지다; 젖혀지다; n. (뾰족한) 끝
If you tip something, you touch it lightly so that it moves in a particular direction.

deliver**
[dilívər]

v. (물건·편지 등을) 배달하다; (사람을) 데리고 가다; (연설·강연 등을) 하다
If you deliver something somewhere, you take it there.

flight of stairs^{복습}

idiom 한 줄로 이어진 계단
A flight of stairs is a set of steps or stairs that lead from one level to another without changing direction.

interrupt**
[intərʌ́pt]

v. (말·행동을) 방해하다, 중단시키다
If you interrupt someone who is speaking, you say or do something that causes them to stop.

count on

idiom 기대하다, 의지하다
If you count on someone, you have confidence in them because you know that they will do what you want.

responsible**
[rispánsəbl]

a. 책임감 있는; (~을) 책임지고 있는; (~에 대해) 책임이 있는
Responsible people behave properly and sensibly, without needing to be supervised.

help yourself

idiom (음식 등을) 마음대로 드시오
If someone tells you to help yourself, they are telling you politely to serve yourself anything you want or to take anything you want.

messenger*
[mésəndʒər]

n. (메시지를 전하는) 전달자, 배달원
A messenger takes a message to someone, or takes messages regularly as their job.

Chapters 8 & 9

1. What was Myron's job as class president?

   A. Myron had to give a speech every morning.

   B. Myron had to turn the lights on and off.

   C. Myron had to take care of students.

   D. Myron had to clean the classroom.

2. How did Myron feel about the job?

   A. He thought that it was important.

   B. He thought that it was hard.

   C. He thought that it was easy.

   D. He thought that it was fun.

3. What did Myron do for Dana after school?

   A. He helped her with her homework.

   B. He helped her make friends at school.

   C. He helped her learn to count.

   D. He helped her bring her dog to the vet.

4. What happened when Myron was late to school the next day?

   A. He had to show the new class president how to work the lights.

   B. He had to apologize to the whole classroom for being late.

   C. He had to check up on Dana at the hospital.

   D. He had forgotten to bring his lunch to school.

5. What was the terrible thing that happened to Maurecia?

    A. She liked everybody in class.

    B. She got tired of ice cream.

    C. She had nothing to eat but ice cream.

    D. She had to work on a project with Kathy.

6. How did Maurecia feel about Maurecia-flavored ice cream?

    A. She thought that it tasted delicious.

    B. She thought that it tasted terrible.

    C. She thought that it tasted like strawberry ice cream.

    D. She thought that it didn't taste like anything at all.

7. Why did liking Todd ice cream turn out to be a problem for Maurecia?

    A. She started to spend more time with Todd.

    B. She could only study if she ate Todd ice cream.

    C. She sometimes tried to take a bite out of Todd's arm.

    D. Nobody like Todd ice cream except for Maurecia.

Check Your Reading Speed

1분에 몇 단어를 읽는지 리딩 속도를 측정해보세요.

$$\frac{663 \text{ words}}{\text{reading time (} \quad \text{) sec}} \times 60 = (\quad) \text{ WPM}$$

Build Your Vocabulary

elect***
[ilékt]

v. (선거로) 선출하다
When people elect someone, they choose that person to represent them, by voting for them.

president***
[prézədənt]

n. 장(長), 회장; 대통령 (class president n. 반장)
The president of an organization is the person who has the highest position in it.

expect복습
[ikspékt]

v. 예상하다, 기대하다
If you expect something to happen, you believe that it will happen.

certain***
[sə:rtn]

a. 확실한, 틀림없는 (certainly ad. 틀림없이, 분명히)
You use certainly to emphasize what you are saying when you are making a statement.

convince*
[kənvíns]

v. 납득시키다, 확신시키다; 설득하다 (convinced a. 확신하는)
If you are convinced that something is true, you feel sure that it is true.

let out

idiom 끝나다
When schools, classes, or offices let out, they come to an end and students or workers go home at the end of a day or a term.

turn out

idiom (전기·난방기를) 끄다; ~인 것으로 드러나다; 모습을 드러내다
If you turn something out, you switch a light or a source of heat off.

flick
[flik]

v. (버튼·스위치를) 탁 누르다; (손가락 등으로) 튀기다; n. 휙 움직임
If you flick a switch, or flick an electrical appliance on or off, you press the switch sharply so that it moves into a different position and works the equipment.

horrible복습
[hɔ́:rəbl]

a. 소름 끼치는, 무시무시한; 지긋지긋한, 끔찍한
You can call something horrible when it causes you to feel great shock, fear, and disgust.

screech*
[skri:ʧ]

v. 끼익 하는 소리를 내다; n. 끼익, 귀에 거슬리는 날카로운 소리
If a vehicle screeches somewhere or if its tires screech, its tires make an unpleasant high-pitched noise on the road.

squeal
[skwi:l]

n. 끼익 하는 소리; v. 끼익 하는 소리를 내다
A squeal is a long, high-pitched sound.

roar*
[rɔ:r]

v. 굉음을 내며 질주하다; 으르렁거리다; 고함치다; n. 포효
If something, usually a vehicle, roars somewhere, it goes there very fast, making a loud noise.

faint* [féint]

a. (빛·소리·냄새 등이) 희미한; v. 실신하다
A faint sound, color, mark, feeling, or quality has very little strength or intensity.

bend* [bend]

v. (bent-bent) (몸이나 머리를) 굽히다, 숙이다; (무엇을) 구부리다; n. 굽이, 굽은 곳
When you bend, you move the top part of your body downward and forward.

matter** [mǽtər]

n. 문제; 관건; 일, 사안; v. 중요하다; 문제되다
You use matter in expressions such as 'What's the matter?' when you think that someone has a problem and you want to know what it is.

sob* [sab]

v. (흑흑) 흐느끼다, 흐느껴 울다; n. 흐느껴 울기, 흐느낌
When someone sobs, they cry in a noisy way, breathing in short breaths.

speed^{복습} [spi:d]

v. (sped/speeded-sped/speeded) 빨리 가다; 더 빠르게 하다, 가속화하다; n. (물체의 이동) 속도
If you speed somewhere, you move or travel there quickly, usually in a vehicle.

unconscious* [ʌnkánʃəs]

a. 의식을 잃은, 의식이 없는; 무의식적인
Someone who is unconscious is in a state similar to sleep, usually as the result of a serious injury or a lack of oxygen.

careful** [kéərfəl]

a. 조심하는, 주의 깊은; 세심한 (carefully ad. 주의하여, 조심스럽게)
If you are careful, you give serious attention to what you are doing, in order to avoid harm, damage, or mistakes.

vet [vet]

n. (= veterinarian) 수의사
A vet is someone who is qualified to treat sick or injured animals.

pet* [pet]

v. (동물·아이를 다정하게) 어루만지다; n. 애완동물
If you pet a person or animal, you touch them in an affectionate way.

lick* [lik]

v. 핥다; 핥아먹다; n. 한 번 핥기, 핥아먹기
When people or animals lick something, they move their tongue across its surface.

in time

idiom 시간 맞춰, 늦지 않게
If you do something in time, you are not too late for doing it.

bite* [bait]

v. (bit-bitten) 물다, 베어 물다;
n. 물기; 한 입 (베어 문 조각); (짐승·곤충에게) 물린 상처
If an animal or person bites you, they use their teeth to hurt or injure you.

medicine* [médəsin]

n. 약, 약물; 의학, 의술, 의료
Medicine is a substance that you drink or swallow in order to cure an illness.

complete** [kəmplí:t]

a. 가능한 최대의, 완벽한; v. 완료하다, 끝마치다 (completely ad. 완전히)
You use complete to emphasize that something is as great in extent, degree, or amount as it possibly can be.

catch on

idiom ~을 이해하다
If you catch on something, you understand it.

Check Your Reading Speed

1분에 몇 단어를 읽는지 리딩 속도를 측정해보세요.

$$\frac{529\ \text{words}}{\text{reading time (}\quad\text{) sec}} \times 60 = (\quad)\ \text{WPM}$$

Build Your Vocabulary

beat^{복습}
[biːt]

v. (아주 세게 계속) 때리다; (게임·시합에서) 이기다; n. 고동, 맥박; 리듬
If you beat someone or something, you hit them very hard.

ripple*
[rípl]

n. 잔물결, 파문; v. 잔물결을 이루다; (감정 등이) 파문처럼 번지다
Ripples are little waves on the surface of water caused by the wind or by something moving in or on the water.

terrible^{복습}
[térəbl]

a. 끔찍한, 소름 끼치는; 형편없는; 극심한, 엄청난
A terrible experience or situation is very serious or very unpleasant.

mess*
[mes]

n. (지저분하고) 엉망진창인 상태; (많은 문제로) 엉망인 상황; v. 엉망으로 만들다
If you say that something is a mess or in a mess, you think that it is in an untidy state.

sticky*
[stíki]

a. 끈적거리는, 끈적끈적한, 달라붙는
A sticky substance is soft, or thick and liquid, and can stick to other things.

flavor*
[fléivər]

n. (음식·술의) 맛; v. 맛을 더하다
The flavor of a food or drink is its taste.

lick^{복습}
[lik]

n. 한 번 핥기, 핥아먹기; v. 핥다; 핥아먹다
A lick is an act of passing your tongue over something.

heartbroken
[háːrtbròukən]

a. 비통해하는
Someone who is heartbroken is very sad and emotionally upset.

creamy
[kríːmi]

a. 크림이 많이 든; 크림 같은
Food or drink that is creamy contains a lot of cream or milk.

slap*
[slæp]

v. (손바닥으로) 철썩 때리다; 털썩 놓다; n. (손바닥으로) 철썩 때리기
If you slap someone, you hit them with the palm of your hand.

turn out^{복습}

idiom ~인 것으로 드러나다; 모습을 드러내다; (전기·난방기를) 끄다
If it turns out that something is the case, it is discovered or proved that it is the case.

every once in a while

idiom 가끔, 이따금
If something happens once in a while, it happens sometimes, but not very often.

bite^{복습}
[bait]

n. 한 입 (베어 문 조각); 물기; (짐승·곤충에게) 물린 상처; v. 물다, 베어 물다
A bite of something, especially food, is the action of biting it.

Chapters 10 & 11

1. Why did Paul think he had the best seat in Mrs. Jewls class?
   A. It was exactly in the middle of the classroom.
   B. It was in the front of the room closest to Mrs. Jewls.
   C. It was in the back of the room farthest away from Mrs. Jewls.
   D. It was in the back of the room with the best view of the blackboard.

2. How did Paul feel about Leslie's pigtails?
   A. Paul wanted to pull one.
   B. Paul wished he had pigtails.
   C. Paul wanted to cut one off.
   D. Paul could easily ignore them.

3. Why did Paul pull the left pigtail even harder than the right one?
   A. He was trying to be funny.
   B. He wanted Leslie to scream louder.
   C. He wanted Leslie to cry.
   D. He thought he hadn't pulled the right one hard enough.

4. Why did Paul think that he could pull Leslie's pigtail everyday?

    A. He sat in the back of class and nobody could see him.

    B. He sat in the back of class and nobody would believe Leslie.

    C. He could pull them twice and stay out of trouble for the rest of the day.

    D. Mrs. Jewls would stop caring as time passed and not write his name on the blackboard.

5. Why did Dana tell Mrs. Jewls that she could not do arithmetic?

    A. She had lost her glasses.

    B. She had forgotten how to count.

    C. She was sick and had missed an earlier class.

    D. She itched all over and couldn't concentrate.

6. How did Mrs. Jewls want to help Dana with her mosquito bites?

    A. She gave Dana calamine lotion.

    B. She turned Dana mosquito bites into number.

    C. She sent Dana to the nurse's office for anti-itch cream.

    D. She told students to help scratch Dana's mosquito bites.

7. Why was Dana glad that her mosquito bites turned into numbers instead of letters?

    A. She could never spell mosquito.

    B. She could never spell itch.

    C. She could never spell scratch.

    D. She could never spell calamine lotion.

Check Your Reading Speed

1분에 몇 단어를 읽는지 리딩 속도를 측정해보세요.

$$\frac{931 \text{ words}}{\text{reading time (} \quad \text{) sec}} \times 60 = (\quad) \text{ WPM}$$

Build Your Vocabulary

fraction
[frǽkʃən]

n. 분수; 부분, 일부
A fraction is a number that can be expressed as a proportion of two whole numbers. For example, 1/2 and 1/3 are both fractions.

blackboard^{복습}
[blǽkbɔ̀:rd]

n. 칠판
A blackboard is a dark-colored board that you can write on with chalk.

pay attention

idiom 관심을 갖다
If you pay attention to someone, you watch them, listen to them, or take notice of them.

pigtail
[pígtèil]

n. (하나 또는 두 갈래로) 땋은 머리
If someone has a pigtail or pigtails, their hair is plaited or braided into one or two lengths.

all the way^{복습}

idiom 내내, 시종; 완전히
You use all the way to emphasize how long a distance is.

waist^{**}
[weist]

n. 허리; (옷의) 허리 부분
Your waist is the middle part of your body where it narrows slightly above your hips.

urge[*]
[ə:rdʒ]

n. (강한) 욕구, 충동; v. (~하도록) 충고하다, 설득하려 하다
If you have an urge to do or have something, you have a strong wish to do or have it.

come over

idiom (어떤 기분이) 갑자기 들다
If a feeling comes over, you suddenly start to feel that way.

wrap^{**}
[ræp]

v. 두르다; (포장지 등으로) 싸다, 포장하다; n. 포장지
If someone wraps their arms, fingers, or legs around something, they put them firmly around it.

fist[*]
[fist]

n. 주먹
Your hand is referred to as your fist when you have bent your fingers in toward the palm in order to hit someone.

yank
[jæŋk]

v. 확 잡아당기다
If you yank someone or something somewhere, you pull them there suddenly and with a lot of force.

tie^{**}
[tai]

v. (끈이나 매듭으로) 묶다; 결부시키다; 구속하다; n. 끈; (강한) 유대[관계]
If you tie two things together or tie them, you fasten them together with a knot.

tell on

idiom ~를 고자질하다
If you tell on someone, you tell a teacher or someone else in authority that they have done something wrong.

sigh 복습
[sai]

v. 한숨을 쉬다, 한숨짓다; n. 한숨
When you sigh, you let out a deep breath, as a way of expressing feelings such as disappointment, tiredness, or pleasure.

withdraw*
[wiðdrɔ́ː]

v. (withdrew-withdrawn) (뒤로) 물러나다, 철수하다
If you withdraw something from a place, you remove it or take it away.

ignore 복습
[ignɔ́ːr]

v. (사람을) 못 본 척하다, 무시하다
If you ignore someone or something, you pay no attention to them.

dangle
[dǽŋgl]

v. (달랑) 매달리다, 달랑거리다
If something dangles from somewhere or if you dangle it somewhere, it hangs or swings loosely.

beg*
[beg]

v. 간청하다, 애원하다; 구걸하다
If you beg someone to do something, you ask them very anxiously or eagerly to do it.

tug*
[tʌg]

n. (갑자기 세게) 잡아당김; v. (세게) 잡아당기다
A tug is a sudden strong pull on something.

foolish***
[fúːliʃ]

a. 어리석은; 바보 같은 (기분이 들게 하는)
If someone's behavior or action is foolish, it is not sensible and shows a lack of good judgment.

matter 복습
[mǽtər]

n. 문제; 관건; 일, 사안; v. 중요하다; 문제되다
You use no matter in expressions such as 'no matter how' to say that something is true or happens in all circumstances.

tempt*
[tempt]

v. (좋지 않은 일을 하도록) 유혹하다; (어떤 것을 제의하거나 하여) 유도하다
(tempting a. 솔깃한, 구미가 당기는)
If something is tempting, it makes you want to do it or have it.

think over

idiom (결정을 내리기 전에) ~을 심사숙고하다
If you think something over, you consider it carefully, especially before making a decision.

shoot 복습
[ʃuːt]

v. (shot-shot) 휙 움직이다; (총 등을) 쏘다; 슛을 하다; n. 촬영
If someone or something shoots in a particular direction, they move in that direction quickly and suddenly.

grab 복습
[græb]

v. (와락·단단히) 붙잡다; ~을 잡으려고 하다; n. 와락 잡아채려고 함
If you grab something, you take it or pick it up suddenly and roughly.

scream 복습
[skriːm]

v. 비명을 지르다, 괴성을 지르다; n. 비명, 절규
When someone screams, they make a very loud, high-pitched cry, because they are in pain or are very frightened.

discipline 복습
[dísəplin]

n. 규율, 훈육; 단련법, 수련법
Discipline is the practice of making people obey rules or standards of behavior, and punishing them when they do not.

satisfy*
[sǽtisfài]

v. 만족시키다; 충족시키다 (satisfied a. 만족하는, 흡족해하는)
If you are satisfied with something, you are happy because you have got what you wanted or needed.

big deal

idiom 그게 무슨 대수라고!
You can say big deal for suggesting that something is not as important or impressive as someone else thinks it is.

no way

idiom 절대로 안 돼; 조금도 ~않다
You can say no way as an emphatic way of saying no.

come on

idiom (독촉·설득·격려의 의미로) 자 어서, 빨리; 등장하다, 시작하다
You say 'come on' to encourage someone to do something, for example, to hurry.

harm**
[ha:rm]

n. 해, 피해, 손해; v. 해치다; 해를 끼치다, 손상시키다
Harm is the damage to something which is caused by a particular course of action.

whine
[hwain]

v. 칭얼거리다, 우는 소리를 하다
If something or someone whines, they make a long, high-pitched noise, especially one which sounds sad or unpleasant.

I bet

idiom 설마 그럴라고(상대방의 말을 믿지 않음을 나타냄); 왜 안 그랬겠어(상대방의 말에 이해를 표할 때 쓰는 표현)
You use 'I bet' to tell someone that you do not believe what they have just said.

cross my heart

idiom 맹세할 수 있다
You can say 'cross my heart' when you want someone to believe that you are telling the truth.

conclude**
[kənklú:d]

v. 끝내다, 마치다; 결론을 내리다
When you conclude, you say the last thing that you are going to say.

erase복습
[iréis]

v. (지우개 등으로) 지우다; (완전히) 없애다
If you erase something such as writing or a mark, you remove it, usually by rubbing it with a cloth.

out of nowhere

idiom 난데없이
If you say that something or someone appears out of nowhere, you mean that they appear suddenly and unexpectedly.

Check Your Reading Speed

1분에 몇 단어를 읽는지 리딩 속도를 측정해보세요.

$$\frac{603 \text{ words}}{\text{reading time (\quad) sec}} \times 60 = (\quad) \text{ WPM}$$

Build Your Vocabulary

creature^{**}
n. (~한) 사람; 생명이 있는 존재, 생물
If you say that someone is a particular type of creature, you are focusing on a particular quality they have.

cover^{복습}
[kávər]
v. 덮다; (감추거나 보호하기 위해) 씌우다, 가리다; 다루다, 포함시키다; n. 덮개
To cover something with or in something else means to put a layer of the second thing over its surface.

mosquito^{*}
[məskí:tou]
n. 모기
Mosquitos are small flying insects which bite people and animals in order to suck their blood.

bite^{복습}
[bait]
n. (짐승·곤충에게) 물린 상처; 물기; 한 입 (베어 문 조각); v. 물다, 베어 물다
A bite is an injury or a mark on your body where an animal, snake, or small insect has bitten you.

yardstick
[já:rdstik]
n. (야드) 자; 기준, 척도
A yardstick is a long, flat tool that is one yard long and is used to measure things.

arithmetic^{복습}
[əríθmətik]
n. 산수, 연산; 산술, 계산
Arithmetic is the part of mathematics that is concerned with the addition, subtraction, multiplication, and division of numbers.

itch^{*}
[itʃ]
v. 가렵다, 가렵게 하다; n. 가려움
When a part of your body itches, you have an unpleasant feeling on your skin that makes you want to scratch.

concentrate^{**}
[kánsəntrèit]
v. (정신을) 집중하다, 전념하다; n. 농축물
If you concentrate on something, you give all your attention to it.

carry^{***}
[kǽri]
v. (더하기에서 수를) 한 자리 올리다; (이동 중에) 들고 있다; 나르다
If you carry a number, you put it into another column when doing addition.

carry on^{복습}
idiom 투덜대다
If someone carry on, they behave in an excited or anxious way that is not controlled.

whine^{복습}
[hwain]
v. 칭얼거리다, 우는 소리를 하다
If something or someone whines, they make a long, high-pitched noise, especially one which sounds sad or unpleasant.

thirsty^{*}
[θə́:rsti]
a. 목이 마른, 갈증이 나는; (~을) 갈망하는
If you are thirsty, you feel a need to drink something.

cure[kjuər] ✱✱

n. 치유하는 약, 치유법; (문제 등의) 해결책; v. (사람·동물을) 낫게 하다
A cure for an illness is a medicine or other treatment that cures the illness.

scratch[skrætʃ] ᵇᵒᵏ

v. (가려운 데를) 긁다; 긁힌 자국을 내다; n. 긁힌 자국
If you scratch yourself, you rub your fingernails against your skin because it is itching.

dose[dous] ✱

n. (약의) 복용량; (어느 정도의) 양, 약간
A dose of medicine or a drug is a measured amount of it which is intended to be taken at one time.

turn into[ᵇᵒᵏ]

idiom (~에서) ~이 되다, ~으로 변하다
To turn or be turned into something means to become that thing.

mess[mes] ᵇᵒᵏ

n. (많은 문제로) 엉망인 상황; (지저분하고) 엉망진창인 상태; v. 엉망으로 만들다
If you say that a situation is a mess, you mean that it is full of trouble or problems.

moan[moun] ✱

v. 투덜거리다, 불평하다; 신음하다; n. 신음; 투덜거림, 불평
To moan means to complain or speak in a way which shows that you are very unhappy.

complain[kəmpléin] ᵇᵒᵏ

v. 불평하다, 항의하다
If you complain about a situation, you say that you are not satisfied with it.

count[kaunt] ᵇᵒᵏ

v. 수를 세다; 계산에 넣다; 중요하다; n. 셈, 계산
When you count, you say all the numbers one after another up to a particular number.

spell[spel] ᵇᵒᵏ

v. (어떤 단어의) 철자를 말하다; 철자를 맞게 쓰다, 맞춤법에 맞게 글을 쓰다
Someone who can spell knows the correct order of letters in words.

48

1. Why did Mrs. Jewls put Joy's name on the blackboard?

   A. She had eaten Dameon's lunch.

   B. She had pulled Leslie's pigtail.

   C. She was talking during class.

   D. She was chewing gum.

2. Why did Joy want to get Jason unstuck from his chair?

   A. She could go home early.

   B. She could go play at recess.

   C. She wouldn't have to go home early.

   D. She wanted to make fun of him even more.

3. How did Joy get Jason unstuck from his chair?

   A. She kissed him on the nose.

   B. She poured ice water on him.

   C. She made the Erics cut his pants off.

   D. She made the Erics hold him upside down.

4. What was Rondi missing?

   A. She was missing her homework.

   B. She was missing her two front teeth.

   C. She was missing her shoes.

   D. She was missing her coat.

5. Why did everyone around Rondi start to laugh?
   A. She fell out of her seat.
   B. She had told a funny joke.
   C. She hadn't told a funny joke.
   D. They thought she had a funny smile.

6. What kind of jokes were the funniest according to Mrs. Jewls?
   A. The ones that remain untold
   B. The ones that are about monkeys
   C. The ones that are about magic bananas
   D. The ones that everyone already knows

7. What did Rondi do to Louis at recess?
   A. She asked for a green ball.
   B. She bit his arm with her missing teeth.
   C. She kicked him for laughing at her.
   D. She screamed and punched him.

Check Your Reading Speed

1분에 몇 단어를 읽는지 리딩 속도를 측정해보세요.

$$\frac{853 \text{ words}}{\text{reading time ( ) sec}} \times 60 = (\quad) \text{ WPM}$$

Build Your Vocabulary

awful 복습
[ɔ́:fəl]

a. (양적으로 많음을 강조하는 의미로) 엄청; 끔찍한, 지독한
You can use awful with noun groups that refer to an amount in order to emphasize how large that amount is.

chew＊
[ʧuː]

v. (음식을) 씹다
If you chew gum or tobacco, you keep biting it and moving it around your mouth to taste the flavor of it. You do not swallow it.

hardly 복습
[há:rdli]

ad. 거의 ~아니다; 거의 ~할 수가 없다; ~하자마자
You use hardly in expressions such as hardly ever, hardly any, and hardly anyone to mean almost never, almost none, or almost no-one.

room＊＊＊
[ru:m]

n. (특정 목적을 위한) 자리; 방, -실
If there is room somewhere, there is enough empty space there for people or things to be fitted in, or for people to move freely or do what they want to.

tongue 복습
[tʌŋ]

n. 혀; 언어; 말버릇, 말씨
Your tongue is the soft movable part inside your mouth which you use for tasting, eating, and speaking.

ashamed＊＊
[əʃéimd]

a. (~여서) 부끄러운, 창피한
If you are ashamed of someone, you feel embarrassed to be connected with them, often because of their appearance or because you disapprove of something they have done.

hop 복습
[hap]

v. 급히 가다; 깡충깡충 뛰다; n. 깡충 뛰기
If you hop somewhere, you move there quickly or suddenly.

glob
[glab]

n. (액체·페인트 같은 물질의) 방울
A glob of something soft or liquid is a small round amount of it.

giggle＊
[gigl]

v. 피식 웃다, 킥킥거리다; n. 피식 웃음, 킥킥거림
If someone giggles, they laugh in a childlike way, because they are amused, nervous, or embarrassed.

kindergarten 복습
[kíndərgà:rtn]

n. 유치원
A kindergarten is an informal kind of school for very young children, where they learn things by playing.

company＊＊＊
[kʌ́mpəni]

n. 함께 있음; 회사; (함께 일하거나 공연하는) 단체
Company is having another person or other people with you, usually when this is pleasant or stops you feeling lonely.

rip*
[rip]

v. (갑자기·거칠게) 찢다; 떼어 내다; n. (길게) 찢어진 곳
When something rips or when you rip it, you tear it forcefully with your hands or with a tool such as a knife.

freeze**
[fri:z]

v. 얼리다; 얼다; (두려움 등으로 몸이) 얼어붙다; n. (임금·가격 등의) 동결
If a liquid or a substance containing a liquid freezes, or if something freezes it, it becomes solid because of low temperatures.

sticky 복습
[stíki]

a. 끈적거리는, 끈적끈적한, 달라붙는
A sticky substance is soft, or thick and liquid, and can stick to other things.

remarkable 복습
[rimáːrkəbl]

a. 놀랄 만한, 놀라운, 주목할 만한
Someone or something that is remarkable is unusual or special in a way that makes people notice them and be surprised or impressed.

undercook
[ʌndərkúk]

v. (음식을) 설익히다, 덜 삶다
If you undercook food, you do not cook it enough.

dish**
[diʃ]

n. 요리; 접시; 설거지감
Food that is prepared in a particular style or combination can be referred to as a dish.

overcook
[òuvərkúk]

v. (음식을) 너무 오래 익히다
If you overcook food, you cook it for longer than necessary, reducing its quality as a result.

specialty
[spéʃəlti]

n. (식당의) 전문 음식; 전문 (분야)
A specialty of a particular place is a special food or product that is always very good there.

bowl**
[boul]

n. 한 그릇(의 양); (우묵한) 그릇, 통
The contents of a bowl can be referred to as a bowl of something.

besides 복습
[bisáidz]

ad. 게다가, 뿐만 아니라; prep. ~외에
Besides is used to emphasize an additional point that you are making, especially one that you consider to be important.

silly 복습
[síli]

a. 어리석은, 바보 같은; n. 바보
If you say that someone or something is silly, you mean that they are foolish, childish, or ridiculous.

leer
[liər]

v. 음흉하게 보다
If someone leers at you, they smile in an unpleasant way, usually because they are sexually interested in you.

beg 복습
[beg]

v. 간청하다, 애원하다; 구걸하다
If you beg someone to do something, you ask them very anxiously or eagerly to do it.

tickle*
[tikl]

v. 간지럼을 태우다; n. 간지럽히기
When you tickle someone, you move your fingers lightly over a sensitive part of their body, often in order to make them laugh.

bucket*
[bʌ́kit]

n. 양동이, 들통
A bucket is a round metal or plastic container with a handle attached to its sides.

plead*
[pli:d]

v. 애원하다
If you plead with someone to do something, you ask them in an intense, emotional way to do it.

drench
[drentʃ]

v. 흠뻑 적시다
To drench something or someone means to make them completely wet.

upside down
[ʌ́psàid dáun]

ad. (아래위가) 거꾸로
If something has been moved upside down, it has been turned round so that the part that is usually lowest is above the part that is usually highest.

ceiling**
[síːliŋ]

n. 천장
A ceiling is the horizontal surface that forms the top part or roof inside a room.

helpless*
[hélplis]

a. 무력한, 속수무책인 (helplessly ad. 어찌해볼 수도 없이)
If you are helpless, you do not have the strength or power to do anything useful or to control or protect yourself.

erase 복습
[iréis]

v. (지우개 등으로) 지우다; (완전히) 없애다
If you erase something such as writing or a mark, you remove it, usually by rubbing it with a cloth.

Check Your Reading Speed
1분에 몇 단어를 읽는지 리딩 속도를 측정해보세요.

$$\frac{657 \text{ words}}{\text{reading time ( ) sec}} \times 60 = (\quad) \text{ WPM}$$

Build Your Vocabulary

adorable
[ədɔ́:rəbl]

a. 사랑스러운
If you say that someone or something is adorable, you are emphasizing that they are very attractive and you feel great affection for them.

insist**
[insíst]

v. 고집하다, 주장하다, 우기다
If you insist that something is the case, you say so very firmly and refuse to say otherwise, even though other people do not believe you.

have had enough

idiom (~라면) 진절머리 난다
If you say that you have had enough, you mean that you are unhappy with a situation and you want it to stop.

horrify
[hɔ́:rəfài]

v. 소름 끼치게 만들다 (horrified a. 겁에 질린, 충격 받은)
If someone is horrified, they feel shocked or disgusted, usually because of something that they have seen or heard.

stare^{복습}
[stɛər]

v. 빤히 쳐다보다, 응시하다; n. 빤히 쳐다보기, 응시
If you stare at someone or something, you look at them for a long time.

amaze^{복습}
[əméiz]

v. (대단히) 놀라게 하다 (amazement n. (대단한) 놀라움)
Amazement is the feeling you have when something surprises you very much.

remain***
[riméin]

v. 계속 ~이다; (없어지지 않고) 남다
If someone or something remains in a particular state or condition, they stay in that state or condition and do not change.

untold
[ʌntóuld]

a. 아무에게도 들려주지 않은; 말로 다 할 수 없는
A thing that is untold, was not told to anyone.

disturb**
[distɔ́:rb]

v. (작업·수면 등을) 방해하다; (제자리에 있는 것을) 건드리다
If you disturb someone, you interrupt what they are doing and upset them.

waste^{복습}
[weist]

v. (돈·시간 등을) 낭비하다; 헛되이 쓰다; n. 쓰레기, 폐기물; 낭비
If you waste something such as time, money, or energy, you use too much of it doing something that is not important or necessary, or is unlikely to succeed.

pay attention 복습

idiom 관심을 갖다
If you pay attention to someone, you watch them, listen to them, or take notice of them.

strict**
[strikt]

a. (규칙 등이) 엄격한, 엄한; 엄밀한
A strict rule or order is very clear and precise or severe and must always be obeyed completely.

slap 복습
[slæp]

v. (손바닥으로) 철썩 때리다; 털썩 놓다; n. (손바닥으로) 철썩 때리기
If you slap someone, you hit them with the palm of your hand.

recess 복습
[risés]

n. (학교의) 쉬는 시간; (의회·위원회 등의) 휴회 기간
A recess is a break between classes at a school.

yard 복습
[jɑːrd]

n. (학교의) 운동장; 마당, 뜰; 정원
A yard is a flat area of concrete or stone that is next to a building and often has a wall around it.

frown*
[fraun]

n. 찡그림, 찌푸림; v. 얼굴을 찌푸리다
A frown is a facial expression that usually shows dislike or displeasure.

come on 복습

idiom (독촉·설득·격려의 의미로) 자 어서, 빨리; 등장하다, 시작하다
You say 'come on' to encourage someone to do something, for example, to hurry.

sock
[sak]

v. 세게 치다, 강타하다; n. 양말
If you sock someone, you hit them with your fist.

stomach**
[stʌ́mək]

n. 복부, 배; 위(胃), 속
You can refer to the front part of your body below your waist as your stomach.

bite 복습
[bait]

v. (bit-bitten) 물다, 베어 물다; (짐승·곤충에게) 물린 상처;
n. 물기; 한 입 (베어 문 조각)
If an animal or person bites you, they use their teeth to hurt or injure you.

1. Why did the whole classroom smell awful on the rainy day?
   A. The windows were closed.
   B. The floors were muddy and wet.
   C. The children wore smelly raincoats.
   D. There was a dead rat in the garbage.

2. Why could nobody tell what the new kid, Sammy, looked like?
   A. He was standing in the dark.
   B. He was wearing a hood over his head.
   C. He was wearing a mask over his face.
   D. He was completely covered by his raincoat.

3. What were dead rats always trying to do?
   A. They were always trying to steal children.
   B. They were always trying to stink up classrooms.
   C. They were always trying to sneak into Mrs. Jewls classroom.
   D. They were always trying to escape from the biology classroom.

4. How did the yellow ball perform?
   A. It didn't bounce and never went where kicked.
   B. It was the bounciest ball on the playground.
   C. It went the farthest when someone kicked it.
   D. It was about as good as the green balls.

5. What was Deedee's problem?

   A. She had trouble getting a green or red ball.

   B. She had trouble getting a spot at lunch.

   C. She had trouble finding friends at recess.

   D. She had trouble counting.

6. How did Deedee manage to solve her problem?

   A. She had her friends save her a spot at lunch.

   B. She dressed like a dead rat to get out of class early.

   C. She had Mrs. Jewls help her learn how to count at recess.

   D. She brought her own green ball to school with her.

7. What did Louis think of Deedee when she called him her best friend?

   A. He never had a best friend until her.

   B. He always wanted to be best friends with someone so clever.

   C. He always wanted to be best friends with a student.

   D. He always wanted to be best friends with a dead rat.

Check Your Reading Speed

1분에 몇 단어를 읽는지 리딩 속도를 측정해보세요.

$$\frac{831 \text{ words}}{\text{reading time (} \quad \text{) sec}} \times 60 = (\qquad) \text{ WPM}$$

Build Your Vocabulary

horrible 복습
[hɔ́:rəbl]

a. 지긋지긋한, 끔찍한; 소름 끼치는, 무시무시한
If you describe something or someone as horrible, you do not like them at all.

stinky
[stíŋki]

a. 악취가 나는; 지독한, 역겨운
If something is stinky, it smells extremely unpleasant.

stink
[stiŋk]

v. (stank/stunk-stunk) (고약한) 냄새가 나다, 악취가 풍기다; n. 악취
To stink means to smell extremely unpleasant.

smelly
[sméli]

a. 냄새 나는
Something that is smelly has an unpleasant smell.

raincoat*
[réinkòut]

n. 비옷
A raincoat is a waterproof coat.

awful 복습
[ɔ́:fəl]

a. 끔찍한, 지독한; (양적으로 많음을 강조하는 의미로) 엄청
If you say that something is awful, you mean that it is extremely unpleasant, shocking, or bad.

complete 복습
[kəmplí:t]

a. 가능한 최대의, 완벽한; v. 완료하다, 끝마치다 (completely ad. 완전히)
You use complete to emphasize that something is as great in extent, degree, or amount as it possibly can be.

frown 복습
[fraun]

n. 찡그림, 찌푸림; v. 얼굴을 찌푸리다
A frown is a facial expression that usually shows dislike or displeasure.

terrible 복습
[térəbl]

a. 끔찍한, 소름 끼치는; 형편없는; 극심한, 엄청난
A terrible experience or situation is very serious or very unpleasant.

exclaim*
[ikskléim]

v. 소리치다, 외치다
If you exclaim, you cry out suddenly in surprise, strong emotion, or pain.

greet**
[gri:t]

v. 맞다, 환영하다
When you greet someone, you say 'Hello' or shake hands with them.

blackboard 복습
[blǽkbɔ̀:rd]

n. 칠판
A blackboard is a dark-colored board that you can write on with chalk.

discipline 복습
[dísəplin]

n. 규율, 훈육; 단련법, 수련법
Discipline is the practice of making people obey rules or standards of behavior, and punishing them when they do not.

reply***
[riplái]
v. 대답하다; 답장을 보내다; n. 대답; 답장
When you reply to something that someone has said or written to you, you say or write an answer to them.

closet*
[klázit]
n. 벽장
A closet is a piece of furniture with doors at the front and shelves inside, which is used for storing things.

windbag
[wíndbæg]
n. 수다쟁이
If you call someone a windbag, you are saying in a fairly rude way that you think they talk a great deal in a boring way.

shy*
[ʃai]
a. 수줍음을 많이 타는, 수줍어하는
A shy person is nervous and uncomfortable in the company of other people.

underneath*
[ʌ̀ndərníːθ]
prep. ~의 밑에, ~의 아래에
If one thing is underneath another, it is directly under it, and may be covered or hidden by it.

exact^{복습}
[igzǽkt]
a. 정확한, 정밀한; 꼼꼼한, 빈틈없는 (exactly ad. 정확히, 꼭, 맞아)
You can use not exactly to show that you mean the opposite of what you are saying.

stick out^{복습}
idiom ~을 내밀다, 튀어나오게 하다
If something is sticking out from a surface or object, it extends up or away from it.

bunch*
[bʌnʧ]
n. (한 무리의) 사람들; 다발, 송이, 묶음
A bunch of people is a group of people who share one or more characteristics or who are doing something together.

screech^{복습}
[skriːʧ]
v. 끼익 하는 소리를 내다; n. 끼익, 귀에 거슬리는 날카로운 소리
When you screech something, you shout it in a loud, unpleasant, high-pitched voice.

rotten*
[ratn]
a. 형편없는, 끔찍한; 썩은, 부패한
If you describe someone as rotten, you are insulting them or criticizing them because you think that they are very unpleasant or unkind.

overpower
[òuvərpáuər]
v. 압도하다, 사로잡다; 제압하다 (overpowering a. 아주 강한)
An overpowering smell or sound is so strong that you cannot smell or hear anything else.

remove**
[rimúːv]
v. (옷 등을) 벗다; 치우다; 없애다, 제거하다
If you remove clothing, you take it off.

hiss*
[his]
v. (화난 어조로) 낮게 말하다; 쉿 하는 소리를 내다; n. 쉿 하는 소리
If you hiss something, you say it forcefully in a whisper.

sneak*
[sniːk]
v. 살금살금 가다; 몰래 하다; a. 기습적인
If you sneak somewhere, you go there very quietly on foot, trying to avoid being seen or heard.

Check Your Reading Speed

1분에 몇 단어를 읽는지 리딩 속도를 측정해보세요.

$$\frac{886 \text{ words}}{\text{reading time ( ) sec}} \times 60 = (\quad) \text{ WPM}$$

Build Your Vocabulary

contain^{복습}
[kəntéin]

v. ~이 들어 있다; (감정을) 억누르다
If writing, speech, or film contains particular information, ideas, or images, it includes them.

solution**
[səlúːʃən]

n. (문제·곤경의) 해법, 해결책
A solution to a problem or difficult situation is a way of dealing with it so that the difficulty is removed.

mousey
[máusi]

a. 소심한, 내성적인; (머리카락이) 쥐갈색인
If you describe someone as mousey, you mean that they are quiet and shy and that people do not notice them.

spell^{복습}
[spel]

v. 철자를 맞게 쓰다, 맞춤법에 맞게 글을 쓰다; (어떤 단어의) 철자를 말하다
(spelling n. 철자법, 맞춤법)
When you spell a word, you write or speak each letter in the word in the correct order.

sign***
[sain]

n. 표지판, 간판; 징후, 조짐; 몸짓, 신호; v. (서류·편지 등에) 서명하다
A sign is a piece of wood, metal, or plastic with words or pictures on it. Signs give you information about something, or give you a warning or an instruction.

notice^{복습}
[nóutis]

v. ~을 의식하다; 주목하다, 관심을 기울이다; n. 신경 씀, 알아챔; 공고문
If you notice something or someone, you become aware of them.

cut across

idiom 가로질러 가다
If you cut across a place, you go through it because it is the shortest route to another place.

bounce*
[bauns]

v. 튀다; 튀기다; n. 튐, 튀어 오름
When an object such as a ball bounces or when you bounce it, it moves upward from a surface or away from it immediately after hitting it.

besides^{복습}
[bisáidz]

prep. ~외에; ad. 게다가, 뿐만 아니라
Besides means other than someone or something.

get rid of

idiom ~을 처리하다, 없애다
When you get rid of someone or something that is annoying you or that you do not want, you make yourself free of them or throw something away.

all the way^{복습}

idiom 내내, 시종; 완전히
You use all the way to emphasize how long a distance is.

62

story^{복습}
[stɔ́ːri]

① n. (건물의) 층 ② n. 이야기
A story of a building is one of its different levels, which is situated above or below other levels.

expect^{복습}
[ikspékt]

v. 예상하다, 기대하다
If you expect something to happen, you believe that it will happen.

compete^{**}
[kəmpíːt]

v. 경쟁하다; (시합·경기 등에서) (~와) 겨루다, (시합 등에) 참가하다
If you compete with someone for something, you try to get it for yourself and stop the other person getting it.

I bet^{복습}

idiom 설마 그럴라고(상대방의 말을 믿지 않음을 나타냄);
왜 안 그랬겠어(상대방의 말에 이해를 표할 때 쓰는 표현)
You use 'I bet' to tell someone that you do not believe what they have just said.

stop dead

idiom (사람·기계가) 갑자기 멈추다
To stop dead means to suddenly stop happening or moving.

thud
[θʌd]

n. 쿵, 퍽, 툭(무거운 것이 떨어질 때 나는 소리)
A thud is a dull sound, such as that which a heavy object makes when it hits something soft.

backwards[*]
[bǽkwərdz]

ad. 뒤로; 거꾸로, 반대 방향으로
If you move or look backwards, you move or look in the direction that your back is facing.

bother^{복습}
[báðər]

v. 신경 쓰다, 애를 쓰다; 귀찮게 하다, 귀찮게 말을 걸다; n. 성가심
If you do not bother to do something or if you do not bother with it, you do not do it, consider it, or use it because you think it is unnecessary or because you are too lazy.

chase^{**}
[tʃeis]

v. 뒤쫓다, 추적하다; (돈·성공 등을) 좇다; n. 추적, 추격
If you chase someone, or chase after them, you run after them or follow them quickly in order to catch or reach them.

disgust[*]
[disgʌ́st]

v. 혐오감을 유발하다, 역겹게 하다; n. 혐오감, 역겨움, 넌더리
(disgusting a. 역겨운, 구역질나는)
If you say that something is disgusting, you mean that you find it completely unacceptable.

subject^{**}
[sʌ́bdʒikt]

n. 학과, 과목; (논의 등의) 주제
A subject is an area of knowledge or study, especially one that you study at school, college, or university.

figure out^{복습}

idiom (생각한 끝에) ~을 이해하다; (양·비용을) 계산하다
If you figure out someone or something, you come to understand them by thinking carefully.

shred[*]
[ʃred]

v. (갈가리) 자르다, 채를 썰다; n. (가늘고 작은) 조각 (shredded a. 잘게 조각난)
If you shred something such as food or paper, you cut it or tear it into very small, narrow pieces.

lunchbox
[lʌ́ntʃbàks]

n. 도시락(통)
A lunchbox is a small container with a lid. You put food such as sandwiches in it to eat for lunch at work or at school.

smear
[smiər]

v. 마구 바르다; 비방하다; n. (기름기 등이 묻은) 얼룩
If you smear a surface with an oily or sticky substance or smear the substance onto the surface, you spread a layer of the substance over the surface.

stuff*
[stʌf]

v. (재빨리·되는대로) 쑤셔 넣다; (빽빽히) 채워 넣다; n. 것(들), 물건, 물질
If you stuff something somewhere, you push it there quickly and roughly.

put out

idiom 화가 나다, 불쾌해하다
If you are put out, you are upset or offended.

immediate**
[imíːdiət]

a. 즉각적인; 당면한; 아주 가까이에 있는 (immediately ad. 즉시, 즉각)
An immediate result, action, or reaction happens or is done without any delay.

instant*
[ínstənt]

a. 즉각적인; n. 순간, 아주 짧은 동안 (instantly ad. 즉각, 즉시)
You use instant to describe something that happens immediately.

playground^{복습}
[pléigràund]

n. (학교의) 운동장; 놀이터
A playground is a piece of land, at school or in a public area, where children can play.

pretend^{복습}
[priténd]

v. ~인 척하다, ~인 것처럼 굴다; ~라고 가장하다
If you pretend that something is the case, you act in a way that is intended to make people believe that it is the case, although in fact it is not.

trick**
[trik]

v. 속이다, 속임수를 쓰다; n. 속임수
If someone tricks you, they deceive you, often in order to make you do something.

kindergarten^{복습}
[kíndərgàːrtn]

n. 유치원
A kindergarten is an informal kind of school for very young children, where they learn things by playing.

insist^{복습}
[insíst]

v. 고집하다, 주장하다, 우기다
If you insist that something is the case, you say so very firmly and refuse to say otherwise, even though other people do not believe you.

you bet

idiom 물론이지, 바로 그거야
You use 'you bet' to say yes in an emphatic way or to emphasize a reply or statement.

terrific*
[tərífik]

a. 아주 좋은, 멋진, 훌륭한; (양·정도 등이) 엄청난
If you describe something or someone as terrific, you are very pleased with them or very impressed by them.

1. Why did Mrs. Jewls stop writing Todd's name on the blackboard?

   A. She saw D.J.'s smile.

   B. She thought of a funny joke.

   C. She decided that she was always mean to Todd.

   D. She meant to write D.J.'s name on the blackboard.

2. Which of the following was NOT one of the guesses for reasons why D.J. was smiling?

   A. He was in love.

   B. It was his birthday.

   C. He had gotten a green ball.

   D. Dameon was his best friend.

3. What did D.J. say about being sad and happy?

   A. People needed reasons to be sad and happy.

   B. People needed a reason to be sad but not to be happy.

   C. People needed a reason to be happy but not to be sad.

   D. People didn't need reasons to be sad or happy.

4. How could John only read words?

   A. He could only read words on a computer.

   B. He could only read words on the blackboard.

   C. He could only read words written upside down.

   D. He could only read words written in books.

5. What did Mrs. Jewls say that John would have to learn?
    A. She said that John would have to learn to read bigger books.
    B. She said that John would have to learn to stand on his head.
    C. She said that John would have to learn to read right side up.
    D. She said that John would have to learn to read on a computer.

6. How did the other students help John?
    A. They held his books for him to read.
    B. They held the blackboard upside down.
    C. They surrounded him to not let him fall.
    D. They hit him on the head.

7. What happened when John fell in the end?
    A. He could read the the blackboard without being upside down.
    B. He could still only read things that were upside down.
    C. He hurt himself and went to the school nurse.
    D. He stopped being friends with Joe after he stood on his head.

Check Your Reading Speed

1분에 몇 단어를 읽는지 리딩 속도를 측정해보세요.

$$\frac{476 \text{ words}}{\text{reading time (   ) sec}} \times 60 = (\quad) \text{ WPM}$$

Build Your Vocabulary

skip*
[skip]

v. 깡충깡충 뛰다; (일을) 거르다; n. 깡충깡충 뛰기
If you skip along, you move almost as if you are dancing, with a series of little jumps from one foot to the other.

flight of stairs^{복습}

idiom 한 줄로 이어진 계단
A flight of stairs is a set of steps or stairs that lead from one level to another without changing direction.

grin**
[grin]

v. 활짝 웃다; n. 활짝 웃음
(grin from ear to ear idiom 입이 귀에 걸리도록 활짝 웃다)
When you grin, you smile broadly.

chin**
[tʃin]

n. 턱
Your chin is the part of your face that is below your mouth and above your neck.

pushover
[púʃòuvər]

n. 만만한 사람; 식은 죽 먹기, 아주 쉬운 일
You say that someone is a pushover when you find it easy to persuade them to do what you want.

chalk^{복습}
[tʃɔːk]

n. 분필
Chalk is a small piece of soft white rock, used for writing or drawing with.

shrug^{복습}
[ʃrʌg]

v. (어깨를) 으쓱하다
If you shrug, you raise your shoulders to show that you are not interested in something or that you do not know or care about something.

toothless
[túːθlis]

a. 이가 없는
You use toothless to describe a person or their smile when they have no teeth.

hardly^{복습}
[háːrdli]

ad. 거의 ~아니다; 거의 ~할 수가 없다; ~하자마자
You use hardly in expressions such as hardly ever, hardly any, and hardly anyone to mean almost never, almost none, or almost no-one.

chuckle*
[tʃʌkl]

v. 빙그레 웃다
When you chuckle, you laugh quietly.

ceiling^{복습}
[síːliŋ]

n. 천장
A ceiling is the horizontal surface that forms the top part or roof inside a room.

68

snicker
[sníkər]

v. 낄낄 웃다, 숨죽여 웃다; n. 낄낄 웃음, 숨죽여 웃는 웃음
If you snicker, you laugh quietly in a disrespectful way, for example at something rude or embarrassing.

slap^{복습}
[slæp]

v. (손바닥으로) 철썩 때리다; 털썩 놓다; n. (손바닥으로) 철썩 때리기
If you slap someone, you hit them with the palm of your hand.

ticklish
[tíkliʃ]

a. (사람이) 간지럼을 잘 타는
Someone who is ticklish is sensitive to being tickled, and laughs as soon as you tickle them.

wastepaper
[wéistpeipər]

n. 휴지 (wastepaper basket n. 휴지통)
Wastepaper is paper discarded after use.

settle down

idiom 진정되다; 정착하다
If you settle down, you become quiet and calm.

wipe*
[waip]

v. 닦다, 훔치다; 지우다; n. (행주·걸레로) 닦기
If you wipe something, you rub its surface to remove dirt or liquid from it.

stretch**
[streʧ]

v. (잡아당겨) 늘이다; (팔·다리의 근육을) 당기다; 펼쳐지다
Something that stretches over an area or distance covers or exists in the whole of that area or distance.

out of shape

idiom 제 모양이 아닌, 형태가 찌그러진; 건강이 안 좋은, 몸매가 엉망인
If something is out of shape, it is no longer in its proper or original shape, for example because it has been damaged or wrongly handled.

nod**
[nad]

v. (고개를) 끄덕이다; n. (고개를) 끄덕임
If you nod, you move your head downward and upward to show that you are answering 'yes' to a question, or to show agreement, understanding, or approval.

Check Your Reading Speed

1분에 몇 단어를 읽는지 리딩 속도를 측정해보세요.

$$\frac{620 \text{ words}}{\text{reading time ( ) sec}} \times 60 = (\quad) \text{ WPM}$$

Build Your Vocabulary

upside down^{복습}
[ápsàid dáun]

ad. (아래위가) 거꾸로
If something has been moved upside down, it has been turned round so that the part that is usually lowest is above the part that is usually highest.

correct^{복습}
[kərékt]

a. 적절한, 옳은; 맞는, 정확한; v. 바로잡다, 정정하다
(correctly ad. 바르게, 정확하게)
The correct thing or method is the thing or method that is required or is most suitable in a particular situation.

spend^{복습}
[spend]

v. (시간을) 보내다; (돈을) 쓰다
If you spend time or energy doing something, you use your time or effort doing it.

besides^{복습}
[bisáidz]

ad. 게다가, 뿐만 아니라; prep. ~외에
Besides is used to emphasize an additional point that you are making, especially one that you consider to be important.

stand^{복습}
[stænd]

v. 서다, 서 있다; 참다, 견디다; 상대하다; n. 태도, 의견
(stand on one's head idiom 물구나무를 서다)
If you stand on your head, you balance upside down with the top of your head and your hands on the ground.

give up^{복습}

idiom 포기하다, 그만두다, 단념하다
If you give up, you decide that you cannot do something and stop trying to do it.

after all^{복습}

idiom 어쨌든; (예상과는 달리) 결국에는
You use after all when introducing a statement which supports or helps explain something you have just said.

nonsense^{**}
[nánsens]

n. 터무니없는 생각, 허튼소리
If you say that something spoken or written is nonsense, you mean that you consider it to be untrue or silly.

swing^{**}
[swiŋ]

v. (swung-swung) 빙 돌(리)다; (전후·좌우로) 흔들(리)다; 휙 움직이다;
n. 흔들기; 휘두르기
If something swings in a particular direction or if you swing it in that direction, it moves in that direction with a smooth, curving movement.

nothing to it

idiom 아주 쉽다, 아무것도 아니다
If you say 'Nothing to it' or 'There is nothing to it' to someone, you mean that it is easy to do something.

pillow[*]
[pílou]

n. 베개
A pillow is a rectangular cushion which you rest your head on when you are in bed.

give a hand

idiom 거들어주다
If you ask someone to give you a hand with something, you are asking them to help you in what you are doing.

surround^{**}
[səráund]

v. 둘러싸다, 에워싸다; 포위하다
If a person or thing is surrounded by something, that thing is situated all around them.

straighten[*]
[streitn]

v. 똑바르게 하다; (자세를) 바로 하다
If you straighten something, you make it tidy or put it in its proper position.

bam
[bæm]

n. 쿵 (부딪치는 소리)
A bam is a sudden loud noise.

warn^{복습}
[wɔːrn]

v. 경고하다, 주의를 주다, 조심하라고 하다
If you warn someone not to do something, you advise them not to do it so that they can avoid possible danger or punishment.

flip[*]
[flip]

v. (너무 화가 나거나 흥분하여) 확 돌아 버리다; 홱 뒤집(히)다, 휙 젖히다
If you flip or flip out, you become very angry, excited or enthusiastic about something.

reward^{**}
[riwɔ́ːrd]

n. 보상; 현상금, 보상금, 사례금; v. 보상하다, 사례하다
A reward is something that you are given, for example because you have behaved well, worked hard, or provided a service to the community.

1. How did Leslie feel about her toes?

    A. She thought they were useful for counting.

    B. She thought they were useful for sucking.

    C. She thought they served no useful purpose.

    D. She thought they could be used to count.

2. What did Dana do with her toes?

    A. She put them in her mouth to suck.

    B. She used them to scratch her legs.

    C. She used them to kick other children.

    D. She used them to pick up things.

3. Why did Leslie not sell her toes to Louis?

    A. She wanted to sell them as a set.

    B. She wanted to sell them to Dana.

    C. She wanted to sell them to Miss Mush.

    D. She wanted to sell them for a dollar each.

4. How did Leslie feel about Louis wanting to buy her pigtails for a dollar each?

    A. She thought that it was a great deal.

    B. She thought that he was crazy.

    C. She thought that he was funny.

    D. She thought that he was pulling her leg.

5. Why did Kathy like Sammy?
   A. She liked dead rats.
   B. She thought he was short.
   C. She thought he was funny.
   D. She thought that he smelled good.

6. Why did Kathy not like Mrs. Jewls?
   A. Mrs. Jewls told her that her cat wouldn't run away, but it actually did run away.
   B. Mrs. Jewls told her that she baked her a delicious cookie, but it actually was terrible.
   C. Mrs. Jewls told her that she could catch a ball, but she actually dropped it.
   D. Mrs. Jewls told her that she could stand on her head, but she actually fell over.

7. What was Kathy's reason for not liking you?
   A. She knows that you thought Sammy was a mean child.
   B. She knows that if you said something, you would be be wrong.
   C. She knows that you like all of the other children better.
   D. She knows that if you ever met her, you wouldn't like her.

Check Your Reading Speed

1분에 몇 단어를 읽는지 리딩 속도를 측정해보세요.

$$\frac{833 \text{ words}}{\text{reading time ( ) sec}} \times 60 = (\quad) \text{ WPM}$$

Build Your Vocabulary

pigtail 복습
[pígtèil]

n. (하나 또는 두 갈래로) 땋은 머리
If someone has a pigtail or pigtails, their hair is plaited or braided into one or two lengths.

count 복습
[kaunt]

v. 수를 세다; 계산에 넣다; 중요하다; n. 셈, 계산
When you count, you say all the numbers one after another up to a particular number.

adorable 복습
[ədɔ́:rəbl]

a. 사랑스러운
If you say that someone or something is adorable, you are emphasizing that they are very attractive and you feel great affection for them.

serve***
[səːrv]

v. 도움이 되다, 기여하다; (식당 등에서 음식을) 제공하다; n. (테니스 등에서) 서브
If something serves as a particular thing or serves a particular purpose, it performs a particular function, which is often not its intended function.

useful***
[júːsfəl]

a. 유용한, 도움이 되는, 쓸모 있는
If something is useful, you can use it to do something or to help you in some way.

suck**
[sʌk]

v. (입에 넣고) 빨다; (액체·공기 등을) 빨아 먹다; 엉망이다, 형편없다
If you suck something, you hold it in your mouth and pull at it with the muscles in your cheeks and tongue, for example in order to get liquid out of it.

recess 복습
[risés]

n. (학교의) 쉬는 시간; (의회·위원회 등의) 휴회 기간
A recess is a break between classes at a school.

scratch 복습
[skrætʃ]

v. (가려운 데를) 긁다; 긁힌 자국을 내다; n. 긁힌 자국
If you scratch yourself, you rub your fingernails against your skin because it is itching.

itch 복습
[itʃ]

v. 가렵다, 가렵게 하다; n. 가려움
When a part of your body itches, you have an unpleasant feeling on your skin that makes you want to scratch.

yard 복습
[jaːrd]

n. (학교의) 운동장; 마당, 뜰; 정원
The yard of the school is the large open area with a hard surface just outside a school building, where the children can play and do other activities.

hop 복습
[hap]

v. 깡충깡충 뛰다; 급히 가다; n. 깡충 뛰기
If you hop, you move along by jumping on one foot.

tug^{복습}
[tʌg]

v. (세게) 잡아당기다; n. (갑자기 세게) 잡아당김
If you tug something or tug at it, you give it a quick and usually strong pull.

take off one's hands

idiom 책임[짐]을 덜다
If someone takes something off your hands, it means that they relieve you of the burden or bother of it.

nickel^{복습}
[níkəl]

n. (미국·캐나다의) 5센트(짜리 동전); (금속 원소) 니켈
In the United States and Canada, a nickel is a coin worth five cents.

apiece
[əpíːs]

ad. 각각, 하나에
If people have a particular number of things apiece, they have that number each.

anyhow[*]
[énihàu]

ad. 어차피, 어쨌든, 아무튼; 되는대로, 아무렇게나
You use anyhow to indicate that a statement explains or supports a previous point.

think over^{복습}

idiom (결정을 내리기 전에) ~을 심사숙고하다
If you think something over, you consider it carefully, especially before making a decision.

offer^{***}
[ɔ́ːfər]

v. 제의하다, 제안하다, 권하다; (이용할 수 있도록) 내놓다; n. 제의, 제안
If you offer a particular amount of money for something, you say that you will pay that much to buy it.

pull one's leg

idiom 놀리다
If you are pulling someone's leg, you are teasing them by telling them something shocking or worrying as a joke.

take up on

idiom (제의·내기 등을) 받아들이다; ~에게 ~에 대해 의문을 제기하다
If you take someone up on something such as an offer or invitation, you accept it that they have made.

furious[*]
[fjúəriəs]

a. 몹시 화가 난; 맹렬한
Someone who is furious is extremely angry.

scrawny
[skrɔ́ːni]

a. 뼈만 앙상한, 가죽만 남은
If you describe a person or animal as scrawny, you mean that they look unattractive because they are so thin.

runt
[rʌnt]

n. (한배에서 태어난 새끼들 중) 제일 작고 약한 녀석
The runt of a group of animals born to the same mother at the same time is the smallest and weakest of them.

call it square

idiom 청산이 끝난 것으로 하다
If you and someone say 'call it square' to each other, you two pronounce that debt or obligation has been paid, balanced, or ended.

dime^{복습}
[daim]

n. (미국·캐나다의) 10센트(짜리 동전)
A dime is an American coin worth ten cents.

nothing doing

idiom 어림도 없다
You can say 'Nothing doing' in order to tell someone that you refuse to do something or refuse their request.

forget it

idiom 생각도 하지 마; 그만 지껄여; 별 거 아냐
You say 'Forget it' in reply to someone as a way of telling them not
to worry or bother about something, or as an emphatic way of
saying no to a suggestion.

fiery[*]
[fáiəri]

a. (분노가) 맹렬한; 불타는 듯한; 불의
If you describe someone as fiery, you mean that they express very
strong emotions, especially anger, in their behavior or speech.

exclaim[복습]
[ikskléim]

v. 소리치다, 외치다
If you exclaim, you cry out suddenly in surprise, strong emotion, or
pain.

Check Your Reading Speed

1분에 몇 단어를 읽는지 리딩 속도를 측정해보세요.

$$\frac{590 \text{ words}}{\text{reading time ( ) sec}} \times 60 = (\quad) \text{ WPM}$$

Build Your Vocabulary

matter ^{복습}
[mǽtər]

n. 일, 사안; 문제; 관건; v. 중요하다; 문제되다
(as a matter of fact idiom 사실은)
The expression 'as a matter of fact' is used when you are telling someone something interesting, new or important.

run away ^{복습}

idiom (~에서) 달아나다
If you run away, you move quickly away from someone or a place or escape from them or there.

feed**
[fiːd]

v. 밥을 먹이다; 먹이를 주다; n. (아기의) 우유; (동물의) 먹이
If you feed a person or animal, you give them food to eat and sometimes actually put it in their mouths.

pet ^{복습}
[pet]

v. (동물·아이를 다정하게) 어루만지다; n. 애완동물
If you pet a person or animal, you touch them in an affectionate way.

lock**
[lak]

v. (자물쇠로) 잠그다; n. 자물쇠
When you lock something such as a door, drawer, or case, you fasten it, usually with a key, so that other people cannot open it.

closet ^{복습}
[klázit]

n. 벽장
A closet is a piece of furniture with doors at the front and shelves inside, which is used for storing things.

catch***
[kæʧ]

n. 캐치볼; 잡기, 포구; v. (움직이는 물체를) 잡다
Catch is a game in which children throw a ball to each other.

insist ^{복습}
[insíst]

v. 고집하다, 주장하다, 우기다
If you insist that something is the case, you say so very firmly and refuse to say otherwise, even though other people do not believe you.

toss ^{복습}
[tɔːs]

v. (가볍게·아무렇게나) 던지다; n. (고개를) 홱 젖히기
If you toss something somewhere, you throw it there lightly, often in a rather careless way.

cheek**
[ʧiːk]

n. 볼, 뺨
Your cheeks are the sides of your face below your eyes.

sob ^{복습}
[sab]

v. (흑흑) 흐느끼다, 흐느껴 울다; n. 흐느껴 울기, 흐느낌
When someone sobs, they cry in a noisy way, breathing in short breaths.

terrible ^{복습}
[térəbl]

a. 형편없는; 끔찍한, 소름 끼치는; 극심한, 엄청난
If something is terrible, it is very bad or of very poor quality.

stink ^{복습}
[stiŋk]

v. (고약한) 냄새가 나다, 악취가 풍기다; n. 악취
To stink means to smell extremely unpleasant.

crayon ^{복습}
[kréian]

n. 크레용
A crayon is a pencil containing colored wax or clay, or a rod of colored wax used for drawing.

cover ^{복습}
[kʌ́vər]

v. 덮다; (감추거나 보호하기 위해) 씌우다, 가리다; 다루다, 포함시키다; n. 덮개
To cover something with or in something else means to put a layer of the second thing over its surface.

dust *
[dʌst]

n. (흙)먼지; v. 먼지를 털다
Dust is very small dry particles of earth or sand.

bite ^{복습}
[bait]

v. (bit-bitten) (베어) 물다; n. 물기; 한 입 (베어 문 조각); (짐승·곤충에게) 물린 상처
If you bite something, you use your teeth to cut into it, for example in order to eat it or break it.

1. How did Louis get the children to let Ron play kickball?

    A. He told them that he would join their game, too.

    B. He told them that they all had to participate to get a grade.

    C. He told them that Ron was the best player in Wayside School.

    D. He told them that they had to share the ball or they couldn't have it.

2. How did they form teams for kickball?

    A. Ron was on one team with the children, and Louis was on his own team.

    B. Ron and Louis were on their own team, and all the other children were on another team.

    C. Ron, Louis, and half of the children were on one team, and the other half were on another team.

    D. Ron was on one team with half of the children, and Louis was on the other team with the other half.

3. Why did Ron think that Louis could not blame him for playing poorly?

    A. Louis was half the team, too.

    B. Louis had never taught Ron how to play kickball.

    C. Ron was playing on an injured leg.

    D. Ron's arm was a lot stronger than his leg.

4. What were the Erics known for at Wayside School?
   A. They were known for being nice.
   B. They were known for being fat.
   C. They were known for being smart.
   D. They were known for being athletic.

5. Why did people think that Eric Bacon was fat?
   A. He was always slow.
   B. He never played sports.
   C. He was always eating bacon.
   D. The other two Erics were fat.

6. How did Eric Fry get the name "Butterfingers?"
   A. His fingers were always covered in butter.
   B. He always dropped things in class.
   C. He caught a ball but dropped it once.
   D. He always liked eating candy in class.

7. Why was it better that all three Erics had nicknames?
   A. They all had the same last name, too.
   B. They thought that it was more interesting.
   C. They knew exactly which Eric was being called.
   D. The other children knew what they were good and bad at doing.

Check Your Reading Speed

1분에 몇 단어를 읽는지 리딩 속도를 측정해보세요.

$$\frac{560 \text{ words}}{\text{reading time ( ) sec}} \times 60 = (\quad) \text{ WPM}$$

Build Your Vocabulary

curly 복습
[kə́:rli]

a. 곱슬곱슬한
If you have curly hair, it means that your hair is made, growing, or arranged in a round or curved shapes.

kickball 복습
[kíkbɔ:l]

n. 발야구
Kickball is an informal game combining elements of baseball and soccer, in which a soccer ball is thrown to a person who kicks it and proceeds to run the bases.

scram
[skræm]

v. 어서 꺼져라
If you say 'scram' to someone, you ask them to leave quickly.

beat it

idiom 꺼져
If you say 'beat it' to someone, you want them to go away immediately.

stomp
[stamp]

v. 쿵쿵거리며 걷다, 발을 구르다
If you stomp somewhere, you walk there with very heavy steps, often because you are angry.

playground 복습
[pléigràund]

n. (학교의) 운동장; 놀이터
A playground is a piece of land, at school or in a public area, where children can play.

field 복습
[fi:ld]

n. 경기장; 들판, 밭; (도서관·실험실 등이 아닌) 현장; v. 수비를 보다
A sports field is an area of grass where sports are played.

beat 복습
[bi:t]

v. (beat-beaten) (게임·시합에서) 이기다; (아주 세게 계속) 때리다; n. 고동, 맥박; 리듬
If you beat someone in a competition or election, you defeat them.

announce 복습
[ənáuns]

v. 발표하다, 알리다; (공공장소에서) 방송으로 알리다
If you announce something, you tell people about it publicly or officially.

**flock*
[flak]

v. (많은 수가) 모이다; n. 무리, 떼
If people flock to a particular place or event, a very large number of them go there, usually because it is pleasant or interesting.

**pitch*
[pitʃ]

v. (야구에서) 투구하다; (힘껏) 내던지다; n. 경기장
In the game of baseball, when you pitch the ball, you throw it to the batter for them to hit it.

stand 복습
[stænd]

v. 상대하다; 서다, 서 있다; 참다, 견디다; n. 태도, 의견
If you stand someone in a sport you compete with them.

murder[**]
[mə́ːrdər]

v. (경기에서 상대를) 묵사발이 되게 하다; 살해하다, 살인하다; n. 살인(죄), 살해
To murder an opponent in a game or sport means to conclusively defeat them.

smash[*]
[smæʃ]

v. 격파하다; 박살내다; 부딪치다, 충돌하다; n. 박살내기
If you smash someone or something, you defeat or destroy them completely.

position[**]
[pəzíʃən]

n. (팀 경기에서 선수의) 위치; 자리, 제자리
In sports, a position is the place where you play on your team, or the responsibilities of someone who plays in that place.

infield
[ínfiːld]

n. (야구·크리켓에서) 내야
In baseball and cricket, the outfield is the area of the field that is within and near the four bases.

home plate
[hóum pleit]

n. 홈플레이트, 본루
In baseball, home plate is the place that the player has to stand next to in order to hit the ball, and the last place they have to touch to score a point.

outfield
[áutfiːld]

n. (야구·크리켓 등에서) 외야
In baseball and cricket, the outfield is the part of the field that is furthest from the batting area.

all the way[복습]

idiom 내내, 시종; 완전히
You use all the way to emphasize how long a distance is.

tag out

idiom (주자를) 터치아웃시키다
In baseball, to tag out means to touch the runner with the ball, and thereby put them out.

trip[***]
[trip]

v. 발을 헛디디다; n. 여행
If you trip when you are walking, you knock your foot against something and fall or nearly fall.

inning
[íniŋ]

n. (야구에서 9회 중의 한) 회
An inning is one of the nine periods that a standard baseball game is divided into. Each team is at bat once in each inning.

blame[**]
[bleim]

v. ~을 탓하다, ~때문으로 보다; n. 책임; 탓
If you blame a person or thing for something bad, you believe or say that they are responsible for it or that they caused it.

punch[*]
[pʌnʧ]

v. 주먹으로 치다; n. 주먹으로 한 대 침
If you punch someone or something, you hit them hard with your fist.

stomach[복습]
[stʌ́mək]

n. 복부, 배; 위(胃), 속
You can refer to the front part of your body below your waist as your stomach.

Check Your Reading Speed

1분에 몇 단어를 읽는지 리딩 속도를 측정해보세요.

$$\frac{554 \text{ words}}{\text{reading time (} \quad \text{) sec}} \times 60 = (\quad) \text{ WPM}$$

Build Your Vocabulary

throughout**
[θru:áut]

prep. 도처에; ~동안 죽, 내내
If you say that something happens or exists throughout a place, you mean that it happens or exists in all parts of that place.

tip ^{복습}
[tip]

v. 기울어지다, 젖혀지다; (어떤 것이 어느 방향으로 가도록) 살짝 건드리다; n. (뾰족한) 끝
If you tip an object or part of your body or if it tips, it moves into a sloping position with one end or side higher than the other.

after all ^{복습}

idiom 어쨌든; (예상과는 달리) 결국에는
You use after all when introducing a statement which supports or helps explain something you have just said.

skinny
[skíni]

a. 깡마른, 비쩍 여윈
A skinny person is extremely thin, often in a way that you find unattractive.

notice ^{복습}
[nóutis]

v. ~을 의식하다; 주목하다, 관심을 기울이다; n. 신경 씀, 알아챔; 공고문
If you notice something or someone, you become aware of them.

insist ^{복습}
[insíst]

v. 고집하다, 주장하다, 우기다
If you insist that something is the case, you say so very firmly and refuse to say otherwise, even though other people do not believe you.

conclude ^{복습}
[kənklú:d]

v. 끝내다, 마치다; 결론을 내리다
When you conclude, you say the last thing that you are going to say.

nickname*
[níknèim]

n. 별명; v. 별명을 붙이다
A nickname is an informal name for someone or something.

athlete*
[ǽθliːt]

n. 운동을 잘 하는 사람, 운동선수
An athlete is a person who does a sport, especially athletics, or track and field events.

solid**
[sálid]

a. 단단한; 고체의; n. 고체, 고형물
A substance that is solid is very hard or firm.

muscle**
[mʌsl]

n. 근육
A muscle is a piece of tissue inside your body which connects two bones and which you use when you make a movement.

84

sport***
[spɔ:rt]

n. 스포츠, 운동, 경기; 승패에 구애받지 않는 사람
Sports are games such as football and basketball and other competitive leisure activities which need physical effort and skill.

clumsy*
[klʌ́mzi]

a. 어설픈; 세련되지 못한
A clumsy person moves or handles things in a careless, awkward way, often so that things are knocked over or broken.

assume**
[əsúːm]

v. (사실일 것으로) 추정하다
If you assume that something is true, you imagine that it is true, sometimes wrongly.

fabulous*
[fǽbjuləs]

a. 기막히게 좋은; 엄청난, 굉장한
If you describe something as fabulous, you are emphasizing that you like it a lot or think that it is very good.

belt**
[belt]

v. 세게 치다, 강타하다; n. 벨트, 허리띠
If someone belts you, they hit you very hard.

race^{복습}
[reis]

v. 급히 가다; 경주하다, 경쟁하다; n. 경주, 달리기 (시합); 경쟁; 인종, 종족
If you race somewhere, you go there as quickly as possible.

midair
[midéər]

n. 공중, 상공
If something happens in midair, it happens in the air, rather than on the ground.

fingertip
[fíŋgərtip]

n. 손가락 끝
Your fingertips are the ends of your fingers.

squirt
[skwə:rt]

v. 재빠르게 움직이다; (액체·가스 등이 가늘게) 찍 나오다; 찍 짜다
If an object squirts, it move suddenly and unpredictably.

expect^{복습}
[ikspékt]

v. 예상하다, 기대하다
If you expect something to happen, you believe that it will happen.

treat***
[tri:t]

v. (특정한 태도로) 대하다; 여기다, 치부하다; n. (대접하는) 특별한 것, 대접, 한턱
If you treat someone or something in a particular way, you behave toward them or deal with them in that way.

equal***
[íːkwəl]

a. 동등한, 평등한; (수·양·가치 등이) 동일한; v. (수·양·가치 등이) 같다, ~이다 (equally ad. 똑같게, 동등하게; 그와 동시에)
If different groups of people have equal rights or are given equal treatment, they have the same rights or are treated the same as each other, however different they are.

lay off

idiom 그만둬, 그만해
If you say lay off to someone, you tell them to stop doing something that irritates or annoys you.

otherwise**
[ʌ́ðərwàiz]

ad. (만약) 그렇지 않으면; 그 외에는; (~와는) 다르게, 달리
You use otherwise after stating a situation or fact, in order to say what the result or consequence would be if this situation or fact was not the case.

Chapters 23 & 24

1. Why did Allison say that she knocked out Rondi's teeth?
   - A. She said it so that she would get in trouble with Mrs. Jewls.
   - B. She said it so that the boys would stop bothering her.
   - C. She said it so that Rondi would be mad at her.
   - D. She said it so that she could go home early.

2. Why did Allison go back to class before the lunch period was over?
   - A. She felt like taking a nap at her desk.
   - B. She wanted to read a book by herself.
   - C. She wanted to bounce a tennis ball.
   - D. She didn't feel like doing anything else.

3. What secret did Mrs. Jewls say Allison learned?
   - A. She learned how to spell "chair."
   - B. She learned that there was a difference between arithmetic and spelling.
   - C. She learned that children are really smarter than their teachers.
   - D. She learned that she was too nice to everyone around her.

4. Why did Mrs. Jewls send Dameon to Louis?
   - A. Dameon needed to help Louis at recess.
   - B. Dameon wanted to get a green ball for recess.
   - C. Dameon needed to borrow a movie from Louis.
   - D. Dameon needed to ask Louis if he wanted to see a movie.

5. What was Dameon's problem when he finally got back to class?

   A. He didn't know where to find his pencil.

   B. He didn't know what to write about turtles.

   C. He didn't have a notebook or a piece of paper.

   D. He didn't know what movie the class had watched.

6. What did Mrs. Jewls want the class to do with their pencils?

   A. She wanted them to give all of their pencils to Dameon.

   B. She wanted them to trade pencils with other students.

   C. She wanted them to write their names on their pencils.

   D. She wanted them to use their pencils for an art project.

7. What did Dameon spend the rest of the day doing?

   A. He spent the rest of class trying to write about movies.

   B. He spent the rest of class trying to write about turtles.

   C. He spent the rest of class watching the movie by himself.

   D. He spent the rest of class trying to write his name on his pencil.

Check Your Reading Speed

1분에 몇 단어를 읽는지 리딩 속도를 측정해보세요.

$$\frac{630 \text{ words}}{\text{reading time ( ) sec}} \times 60 = (\quad) \text{ WPM}$$

Build Your Vocabulary

blonde*
[bland]
a. (머리가) 금발인; n. 금발 머리 여자
A woman who has blonde hair has pale-colored hair.

windbreaker
[wíndbrèikər]
n. 방한용 재킷
A windbreaker is a warm casual jacket.

knock복습
[nak]
v. (때리거나 타격을 가해) ~한 상태가 되게 만들다; (문 등을) 두드리다;
n. 문 두드리는 소리
If you knock something, you touch or hit it roughly, especially so that it falls or moves.

tease*
[tiːz]
v. 놀리다, 장난하다; n. 남을 놀리기 좋아하는 사람; 장난, 놀림
To tease someone means to laugh at them or make jokes about them in order to embarrass, annoy, or upset them.

bother복습
[báðər]
v. 귀찮게 하다, 귀찮게 말을 걸다; 신경 쓰다, 애를 쓰다; n. 성가심
If someone bothers you, they talk to you when you want to be left alone or interrupt you when you are busy.

peel*
[piːl]
v. (과일·채소 등의) 껍질을 벗기다; 껍질이 벗겨지다; n. (과일·채소의) 껍질
When you peel fruit or vegetables, you remove their skins.

shove*
[ʃʌv]
v. (거칠게) 떠밀다; 아무렇게나 놓다; n. 힘껏 밀침
If you shove someone or something, you push them with a quick, violent movement.

swallow**
[swálou]
v. (음식 등을) 삼키다; 마른침을 삼키다; n. 제비
If you swallow something, you cause it to go from your mouth down into your stomach.

lunchroom
[lʌ́nʧruːm]
n. (학교·회사 등의) 구내식당
A lunchroom is the room in a school or company where you buy and eat your lunch.

story복습
[stɔ́ːri]
① n. (건물의) 층 ② n. 이야기
A story of a building is one of its different levels, which is situated above or below other levels.

librarian*
[laibréəriən]
n. (도서관의) 사서
A librarian is a person who is in charge of a library or who has been specially trained to work in a library.

favor***
[féivər]
n. 호의, 친절; 지지, 인정; v. 선호하다
If you do someone a favor, you do something for them even though you do not have to.

freeze^{복습}
[fri:z]

v. (두려움 등으로 몸이) 얼어붙다; 얼리다; 얼다; n. (임금·가격 등의) 동결
If someone who is moving freezes, they suddenly stop and become completely still and quiet.

tag[*]
[tæg]

n. 잡기 놀이; 꼬리표; v. 꼬리표를 붙이다; 붙잡다
Tag is a game for children in which one child chases the others and tries to touch one of them, who then is the one who chases the children.

bounce^{복습}
[bauns]

v. 튀기다; 튀다; n. 튐, 튀어 오름
When an object such as a ball bounces or when you bounce it, it moves upward from a surface or away from it immediately after hitting it.

chase^{복습}
[tʃeis]

v. 뒤쫓다, 추적하다; (돈·성공 등을) 좇다; n. 추적, 추격
If you chase someone, or chase after them, you run after them or follow them quickly in order to catch or reach them.

shrug^{복습}
[ʃrʌg]

v. (어깨를) 으쓱하다
If you shrug, you raise your shoulders to show that you are not interested in something or that you do not know or care about something.

flight of stairs^{복습}

idiom 한 줄로 이어진 계단
A flight of stairs is a set of steps or stairs that lead from one level to another without changing direction.

period^{복습}
[píːəriəd]

n. (학교의 일과를 나눠 놓은) 시간; 기간, 시기; 마침표
At a school or college, a period is one of the parts that the day is divided into during which lessons or other activities take place.

yard^{복습}
[jaːrd]

n. (학교의) 운동장; 마당, 뜰; 정원
A yard is a flat area of concrete or stone that is next to a building and often has a wall around it.

arithmetic^{복습}
[əríθmətik]

n. 산수, 연산; 산술, 계산
Arithmetic is the part of mathematics that is concerned with the addition, subtraction, multiplication, and division of numbers.

spell^{복습}
[spel]

v. (어떤 단어의) 철자를 말하다; 철자를 맞게 쓰다, 맞춤법에 맞게 글을 쓰다
Someone who can spell knows the correct order of letters in words.

mix up

idiom 혼동하다
If you mix up two or more people or things, you unable to distinguish between them.

Check Your Reading Speed

1분에 몇 단어를 읽는지 리딩 속도를 측정해보세요.

$$\frac{665 \text{ words}}{\text{reading time (\quad) sec}} \times 60 = (\qquad) \text{ WPM}$$

Build Your Vocabulary

hazel
[héizəl]
a. (눈의 색깔이) 녹갈색인; n. 개암나무
Hazel eyes are greenish-brown in color.

dot*
[dat]
n. 점; v. 점을 찍다; 여기저기 흩어져 있다, 산재하다
A dot is a very small round mark or spot.

pupil**
[pjuːpl]
n. 눈동자, 동공; 학생
The pupils of your eyes are the small, round, black holes in the center of them.

turn out 복습
idiom (전기·난방기를) 끄다; ~인 것으로 드러나다; 모습을 드러내다
If you turn something out, you switch a light or a source of heat off.

downstairs**
[dàunstéərz]
ad. 아래층으로; n. 아래층
If you go downstairs in a building, you go down a staircase toward the ground floor.

playground 복습
[pléigràund]
n. (학교의) 운동장; 놀이터
A playground is a piece of land, at school or in a public area, where children can play.

hook**
[huk]
v. ~에 걸다; 갈고리로 잠그다; n. (갈)고리, 걸이
If you hook one thing to another, you attach it there using a hook.

rub**
[rʌb]
v. 문지르다; (두 손 등을) 맞비비다; n. 문지르기, 비비기
If you rub a part of your body, you move your hand or fingers backward and forward over it while pressing firmly.

chin 복습
[ʧin]
n. 턱
Your chin is the part of your face that is below your mouth and above your neck.

shrug 복습
[ʃrʌg]
v. (어깨를) 으쓱하다
If you shrug, you raise your shoulders to show that you are not interested in something or that you do not know or care about something.

all the way 복습
idiom 내내, 시종; 완전히
You use all the way to emphasize how long a distance is.

turtle*
[təːrtl]
n. (바다) 거북
A turtle is a large reptile which has a thick shell covering its body and which lives in the sea most of the time.

rush[**]
[rʌʃ]

v. 급(속)히 움직이다, (너무 급히) 서두르다; n. 혼잡, 분주함
If you rush somewhere, you go there quickly.

sore[**]
[sɔːr]

a. 아픈, 따가운; n. 상처
If part of your body is sore, it causes you pain and discomfort.

hardly[복습]
[háːrdli]

ad. 거의 ~할 수가 없다; 거의 ~아니다; ~하자마자
When you say you can hardly do something, you are emphasizing that it is very difficult for you to do it.

side[***]
[said]

n. (사람 몸통의) 옆구리; (좌우 절반 중 한) 쪽; (아래위나 바닥이 아닌) 옆
Your sides are the parts of your body between your front and your back, from under your arms to your hips.

ache[*]
[eik]

v. (계속) 아프다; n. (계속적인) 아픔
If you ache or a part of your body aches, you feel a steady, fairly strong pain.

matter[복습]
[mǽtər]

n. 문제; 관건; 일, 사안; v. 중요하다; 문제되다
You use matter in expressions such as 'What's the matter?' or 'Is anything the matter?' when you think that someone has a problem and you want to know what it is.

erase[복습]
[iréis]

v. (지우개 등으로) 지우다; (완전히) 없애다 (eraser n. 고무 지우개)
An eraser is an object, usually a piece of rubber or plastic, which is used for removing something that has been written using a pencil or a pen.

blackboard[복습]
[blǽkbɔ̀ːrd]

n. 칠판
A blackboard is a dark-colored board that you can write on with chalk.

waste[복습]
[weist]

n. 쓰레기, 폐기물; 낭비; v. (돈·시간 등을) 낭비하다; 헛되이 쓰다
(waste basket n. 휴지통)
Waste is material which has been used and is no longer wanted, for example because the valuable or useful part of it has been taken out.

fortunate[**]
[fɔ́ːrtʃənət]

a. 운 좋은, 다행한 (fortunately ad. 다행스럽게도, 운이 좋게도)
Fortunately is used to introduce or indicate a statement about an event or situation that is good.

hand[복습]
[hænd]

v. 건네주다, 넘겨주다; n. 손
If you hand something to someone, you pass it to them.

mix-up
[míks-ʌ̀p]

n. (실수로 인한) 혼동
A mix-up is a mistake or a failure in the way that something has been planned.

spend[복습]
[spend]

v. (spent-spent) (시간을) 보내다; (돈을) 쓰다
If you spend time or energy doing something, you use your time or effort doing it.

Chapters 25 & 26

1. How did Jenny come to school?
   A. She took the city bus.
   B. She took the school bus.
   C. She rode in the back of her mother's car.
   D. She rode the back of her father's motorcycle.

2. Why was Jenny worried that the class may have gone on a field trip?
   A. Mrs. Jewls had left a note on the door.
   B. She had seen a school bus going to the park.
   C. Nobody was in the classroom when she arrived.
   D. There were only a few other children in class.

3. Which of the following was NOT something that the man in the mustache said a child would do when nobody was at school?
   A. They might go home.
   B. They might walk around.
   C. They might play games.
   D. They might work on spelling.

4. Why was nobody in class except Jenny?

   A. She had come to school too early.

   B. She had come to school on a Saturday.

   C. All of the other children were sick at home.

   D. All of the other children were on a field trip.

5. How was Terrence at playing sports?

   A. He was a bad sport.

   B. He was a bad athlete.

   C. He didn't play sports.

   D. He only played team sports.

6. Why did the other children not want to play with Terrence?

   A. Terrence smelled bad.

   B. Terrence was too slow.

   C. Terrence always kicked the ball over the fence.

   D. Terrence always ran away after stealing their ball.

7. What did Louis let Terrence have in the end?

   A. He let Terrence have a green ball.

   B. He let Terrence have a yellow ball.

   C. He let the other children kick Terrence.

   D. He let Terrence have a kick over the fence.

Check Your Reading Speed

1분에 몇 단어를 읽는지 리딩 속도를 측정해보세요.

$$\frac{784 \text{ words}}{\text{reading time ( ) sec}} \times 60 = (\text{) WPM}$$

Build Your Vocabulary

motorcycle
[móutərsàikl]
n. 오토바이
A motorcycle is a vehicle with two wheels and an engine.

flight of stairs 복습
idiom 한 줄로 이어진 계단
A flight of stairs is a set of steps or stairs that lead from one level to another without changing direction.

exact 복습
[igzǽkt]
a. 정확한, 정밀한; 꼼꼼한, 빈틈없는 (exactly ad. 정확히, 꼭; 맞아)
You use exactly before an amount, number, or position to emphasize that it is no more, no less, or no different from what you are stating.

field 복습
[fi:ld]
n. (도서관·실험실 등이 아닌) 현장; 들판, 밭; 경기장; v. 수비를 보다 (field trip n. 현장 학습)
A field trip is a visit made by students to study something away from their school or college.

trip 복습
[trip]
n. 여행; v. 발을 헛디디다
A trip is a journey that you make to a particular place.

catch up
idiom (정도나 수준이 앞선 것을) 따라잡다; (먼저 간 사람을) 따라가다
If you catch up on something, you spend extra time doing all the work or tasks that you should have done earlier.

spell 복습
[spel]
v. 철자를 맞게 쓰다, 맞춤법에 맞게 글을 쓰다; (어떤 단어의) 철자를 말하다 (spelling n. 철자법, 맞춤법)
When you spell a word, you write or speak each letter in the word in the correct order.

footstep*
[fútstep]
n. 발소리; 발자국
A footstep is the sound or mark that is made by someone walking each time their foot touches the ground.

hack
[hæk]
v. (마구·거칠게) 자르다, 난도질하다; (컴퓨터) 해킹하다
If you hack something or hack at it, you cut it with strong, rough strokes using a sharp tool such as an ax or knife.

smack*
[smæk]
v. (손바닥으로) 때리다; 탁 소리가 나게 치다; n. 때리기, 후려치기
If you smack someone, you hit them with your hand.

gasp*
[gæsp]
v. 숨이 턱 막히다, 헉 하고 숨을 쉬다; n. (숨이 막히는 듯) 헉 하는 소리를 냄
When you gasp, you take a short quick breath through your mouth, especially when you are surprised, shocked, or in pain.

mustache*
[mʌ́stæʃ]

n. 콧수염
A man's mustache is the hair that grows on his upper lip.

attaché case
[ətǽʃei kèis]

n. (작은) 서류 가방
An attaché case is a flat case for holding documents.

remove^{복습}
[rimúːv]

v. 치우다; (옷 등을) 벗다; 없애다, 제거하다
If you remove something from a place, you take it away.

whisper^{복습}
[hwíspər]

v. 속삭이다, 소곤거리다, 귓속말을 하다; n. 속삭임, 소곤거리는 소리
When you whisper, you say something very quietly.

puzzle*
[pʌzl]

v. 어리둥절하게 하다; n. 퍼즐 (puzzled a. 어리둥절해하는, 얼떨떨한)
Someone who is puzzled is confused because they do not understand something.

concern**
[kənsə́ːrn]

v. ~를 걱정스럽게 만들다; n. 우려, 걱정 (concerned a. 걱정하는)
If something concerns you, it worries you.

certain^{복습}
[sə́ːrtn]

a. 확실한, 틀림없는 (certainly ad. 틀림없이, 분명히)
You use certainly to emphasize what you are saying when you are making a statement.

ride***
[raid]

v. (자전거·오토바이 등을) 타다; (말을) 타다; n. (차량·자전거 등을) 타고 달리기
When you ride a bicycle or a motorcycle, you sit on it, control it, and travel along on it.

bald*
[bɔːld]

a. 대머리의, 머리가 벗겨진
Someone who is bald has little or no hair on the top of their head.

frighten**
[fraitn]

v. 겁먹게 하다, 놀라게 하다 (frightened a. 겁먹은, 무서워하는)
If you are frightened, you are anxious or afraid, often because of something that has just happened or that you think may happen.

newcomer*
[njúːkʌ̀mər]

n. 새로 온 사람, 신입
A newcomer is a person who has recently arrived in a place, joined an organization, or started a new activity.

claim***
[kleim]

v. (~이 사실이라고) 주장하다; 요구하다; n. 주장
If you say that someone claims that something is true, you mean they say that it is true but you are not sure whether or not they are telling the truth.

hand^{복습}
[hænd]

v. 건네주다, 넘겨주다; n. 손
If you hand something to someone, you pass it to them.

satisfy^{복습}
[sǽtisfài]

v. 만족시키다; 충족시키다 (satisfied a. 만족하는, 흡족해하는)
If you are satisfied with something, you are happy because you have got what you wanted or needed.

Check Your Reading Speed

1분에 몇 단어를 읽는지 리딩 속도를 측정해보세요.

$$\frac{717 \text{ words}}{\text{reading time ( ) sec}} \times 60 = (\quad) \text{ WPM}$$

Build Your Vocabulary

athlete^{복습}
[ǽθliːt]

n. 운동을 잘 하는 사람, 운동선수
An athlete is a person who does a sport, especially athletics, or track and field events.

sport^{복습}
[spɔːrt]

n. 승패에 구애받지 않는 사람; 스포츠, 운동, 경기
A sport is a person who has a good attitude about playing a game or having to do something.

reply^{복습}
[riplái]

v. 대답하다; 답장을 보내다; n. 대답; 답장
When you reply to something that someone has said or written to you, you say or write an answer to them.

bounce^{복습}
[bauns]

v. 튀기다; 튀다; n. 튐, 튀어 오름
When an object such as a ball bounces or when you bounce it, it moves upward from a surface or away from it immediately after hitting it.

fence**
[fens]

n. 울타리; 장애물
A fence is a barrier between two areas of land, made of wood or wire supported by posts.

get lost

idiom 꺼져; (거절을 나타내어) 턱도 없어
If you say 'get lost' to someone, you tell them to go away in an impolite way.

take a shot^{복습}

idiom (농구·축구에서) 슛을 하다; 시도하다
If you take a shot, you attempt to score a point by throwing, hitting, or kicking a ball.

hoop
[huːp]

n. (농구의) 링; (금속·나무·플라스틱으로 만든 큰) 테
A hoop is the round metal rim from which a basketball net is suspended.

underhand
[ʌ́ndərhænd]

a. 밑으로 던지는; 비밀의, 부정직한
You use underhand to describe actions, such as throwing a ball, in which you do not raise your arm above your shoulder.

way^{복습}
[wei]

ad. 아주 멀리; 큰 차이로, 훨씬; n. 방법, 방식; (어떤 곳에 이르는) 길
You can use way to emphasize, for example, that something is a great distance away or is very much below or above a particular level or amount.

rim*
[rim]

n. (둥근 물건의) 가장자리, 테두리; v. 둘러싸다, 테를 두르다
The rim of a circular object is its outside edge.

idiot
[ídiət]

n. 바보, 멍청이
If you call someone an idiot, you are showing that you think they are very stupid or have done something very stupid.

no way^{복습}

idiom 절대로 안 돼; 절대로 안 되다, 싫다; 조금도 ~않다
You can say no way as an emphatic way of saying no.

newcomer^{복습}
[njúːkʌmər]

n. 새로 온 사람, 신입
A newcomer is a person who has recently arrived in a place, joined an organization, or started a new activity.

yell[*]
[jel]

v. 고함치다, 소리 지르다; n. 고함, 외침
If you yell, you shout loudly, usually because you are excited, angry, or in pain.

warthog
[wɔ́ːrthàːg]

n. 혹멧돼지
A warthog is a wild pig with two large teeth that curve upward at the sides of its mouth.

mysterious^{**}
[mistíəriəs]

a. 이해하기 힘든, 기이한, 불가사의한 (mysteriously ad. 이상하게)
Someone or something that is mysterious is strange and is not known about or understood.

nod^{복습}
[nad]

v. (고개를) 끄덕이다; n. (고개를) 끄덕임
If you nod, you move your head downward and upward to show that you are answering 'yes' to a question, or to show agreement, understanding, or approval.

demand^{복습}
[dimǽnd]

v. 요구하다; 강력히 묻다, 따지다; n. 요구 (사항); 수요
If you demand something such as information or action, you ask for it in a very forceful way.

deserve^{***}
[dizɔ́ːrv]

v. ~을 (당)해야 마땅하다, ~을 누릴 자격이 있다
If you say that a person or thing deserves something, you mean that they should have it or receive it because of their actions or qualities.

definite^{**}
[défənit]

a. 분명한, 뚜렷한; 확실한, 확고한 (definitely ad. 분명히, 틀림없이)
You use definitely to emphasize that something is the case, or to emphasize the strength of your intention or opinion.

come on^{복습}

idiom (독촉·설득·격려의 의미로) 자 어서, 빨리; 등장하다, 시작하다
You say 'come on' to encourage someone to do something, for example, to hurry.

recess^{복습}
[risés]

n. (학교의) 쉬는 시간; (의회·위원회 등의) 휴회 기간
A recess is a break between classes at a school.

Chapters 27 & 28

1. Why was Joy hungry at lunchtime?

    A. She had worked too hard studying.

    B. She had played too hard in the morning.

    C. She had forgotten her lunch at home.

    D. She had already eaten her lunch during class.

2. Why did Dameon leave his lunch on his desk?

    A. He wanted someone else to take it.

    B. He went to get milk from Miss Mush.

    C. He went to wash his hands in the bathroom.

    D. He went to go get a school lunch instead.

3. How did Dameon feel when Joy offered her lunch to him?

    A. He thanked her and thought she was the best.

    B. He thanked her and wanted to share it with her.

    C. He suspected her of stealing and eating his lunch.

    D. He thought that he should have gotten lunch from Miss Mush.

4. How did Nancy feel about his name?

    A. He thought it was a fancy name.

    B. He thought it was a girl's name.

    C. He thought it was a pet's name.

    D. He thought it was an old person's name.

5. Why were Nancy and the girl on the twenty-third story friends?

   A. They both had girl names.

   B. They both had boy names.

   C. They didn't know each other's names.

   D. They liked playing the same games together.

6. How did Nancy and Mac trade names?

   A. They traded spots in each other's classroom.

   B. They wiggled their ears and stuck out their tongues.

   C. They went to Mrs. Jewls to have her trade their names.

   D. They spun around one hundred times in opposite directions.

7. Why did the children decide to keep their own names in the end?

   A. It made things easier.

   B. The children liked them after all.

   C. Everyone wanted to be Mrs. Jewls.

   D. They forgot which Eric was which.

Check Your Reading Speed

1분에 몇 단어를 읽는지 리딩 속도를 측정해보세요.

$$\frac{736 \text{ words}}{\text{reading time (\quad) sec}} \times 60 = (\quad) \text{ WPM}$$

Build Your Vocabulary

lunchtime
[lʌ́nʧtàim]

n. 점심 시간
Lunchtime is the period of the day when people have their lunch.

meal***
[mi:l]

n. 식사, 끼니 (meal ticket n. 식권)
A meal is an occasion when people sit down and eat, usually at a regular time.

terrible^{복습}
[térəbl]

a. 극심한, 엄청난; 끔찍한, 소름 끼치는; 형편없는 (terribly ad. 몹시, 극심하게)
You use terrible to emphasize the great extent or degree of something.

sack*
[sæk]

n. (종이) 봉지, 부대
A sack is a paper or plastic bag, which is used to carry things bought in a food shop.

turkey*
[tə́:rki]

n. 칠면조 (고기)
A turkey is a large bird that is kept on a farm for its meat.

crisp*
[krisp]

a. (야채·과일 등이) 아삭아삭한, 신선한; (식품이) 바삭바삭한; n. 감자칩
Food that is crisp is pleasantly hard, or has a pleasantly hard surface.

ruin**
[ru:in]

v. 망치다, 엉망으로 만들다; n. 붕괴, 몰락
To ruin something means to severely harm, damage, or spoil it.

waste^{복습}
[weist]

v. (돈·시간 등을) 낭비하다; 헛되이 쓰다; n. 쓰레기, 폐기물; 낭비
If you waste something such as time, money, or energy, you use too much of it doing something that is not important or necessary, or is unlikely to succeed.

spot^{복습}
[spat]

v. 발견하다, 찾다, 알아채다; n. (작은) 점, 반점
If you spot something or someone, you notice them.

notice^{복습}
[nóutis]

v. ~을 의식하다; 주목하다, 관심을 기울이다; n. 신경 씀, 알아챔; 공고문
If you notice something or someone, you become aware of them.

have second thoughts

idiom 다시 생각한 후 마음을 바꾸다
If you have second thoughts, you change your opinion about something or have doubts about it.

grab^{복습}
[græb]

v. (와락·단단히) 붙잡다; ~을 잡으려고 하다; n. 와락 잡아채려고 함
If you grab something, you take it or pick it up suddenly and roughly.

100

wrap ^{복습}
[ræp]

v. (포장지 등으로) 싸다, 포장하다; 두르다; n. 포장지
When you wrap something, you fold paper or cloth tightly round it to cover it completely, for example in order to protect it or so that you can give it to someone as a present.

core[*]
[kɔːr]

n. (사과 같은 과일의) 속; (사물의) 중심부; 핵심
The core of a fruit is the central part of it.

ashamed ^{복습}
[əʃéimd]

a. (~여서) 부끄러운, 창피한
If you are ashamed of someone, you feel embarrassed to be connected with them, often because of their appearance or because you disapprove of something they have done.

discipline ^{복습}
[dísəplin]

n. 규율, 훈육; 단련법, 수련법
Discipline is the practice of making people obey rules or standards of behavior, and punishing them when they do not.

announce ^{복습}
[ənáuns]

v. 발표하다, 알리다; (공공장소에서) 방송으로 알리다
If you announce something, you tell people about it publicly or officially.

stand firm

idiom (의견을 바꾸지 않고) 완강히 버티다
If someone stands firm, they refuse to change their mind about something.

evidence[*]
[évədəns]

n. 증거, 흔적; v. 증언하다
Evidence is anything that you see, experience, read, or are told that causes you to believe that something is true or has really happened.

ought to ^{복습}

idiom ~해야 한다; ~할 필요가 있다; ~일 것이다
You use 'ought to' to mean that it is morally right to do a particular thing or that it is morally right for a particular situation to exist, especially when giving or asking for advice or opinions.

solve^{**}
[salv]

v. (수학 문제 등을) 풀다; (문제·곤경을) 해결하다
If you solve a problem or a question, you find a solution or an answer to it.

yard ^{복습}
[jaːrd]

n. (학교의) 운동장; 마당, 뜰; 정원
A yard is a flat area of concrete or stone that is next to a building and often has a wall around it.

dried-up
[draid-ʌp]

a. 바싹 마른; (늙어서) 쭈글쭈글한
If you describe something as dried-up, you mean that it is dry and has no moisture on it.

detective[*]
[ditéktiv]

n. 탐정; 형사, 수사관
A detective is someone whose job is to discover what has happened in a crime or other situation and to find the people involved.

generous^{**}
[dʒénərəs]

a. (무엇을 주는 데 있어서) 후한; 넉넉한
A generous person gives more of something, especially money, than is usual or expected.

help yourself ^{복습}

idiom (음식 등을) 마음대로 드시오

If someone tells you to help yourself, they are telling you politely to serve yourself anything you want or to take anything you want.

erase ^{복습}
[iréis]

v. (지우개 등으로) 지우다; (완전히) 없애다

If you erase something such as writing or a mark, you remove it, usually by rubbing it with a cloth.

lousy
[láuzi]

a. (아주) 안 좋은, 엉망인

If you describe something as lousy, you mean that it is of very bad quality or that you do not like it.

dinnertime
[dínərtàim]

n. 저녁 식사 시간

Dinnertime is the period of the day when most people have their dinner.

horrible ^{복습}
[hɔ́:rəbl

a. 지긋지긋한, 끔찍한; 소름 끼치는, 무시무시한

Horrible is used to emphasize how bad something is.

filch
[filʧ]

v. 좀도둑질하다

If you say that someone filches something, you mean they steal it, especially when you do not consider this to be a very serious crime.

Check Your Reading Speed

1분에 몇 단어를 읽는지 리딩 속도를 측정해보세요.

$$\frac{742 \text{ words}}{\text{reading time (} \quad \text{) sec}} \times 60 = (\quad) \text{ WPM}$$

Build Your Vocabulary

odd**
[ad]

a. 이상한, 특이한; 홀수의
If you describe someone or something as odd, you think that they are strange or unusual.

shy 복습
[ʃai]

a. 수줍음을 많이 타는, 수줍어하는
A shy person is nervous and uncomfortable in the company of other people.

ashamed 복습
[əʃéimd]

a. (~여서) 부끄러운, 창피한
If someone is ashamed, they feel embarrassed or guilty because of something they do or they have done, or because of their appearance.

story 복습
[stɔ́:ri]

① n. (건물의) 층 ② n. 이야기
A story of a building is one of its different levels, which is situated above or below other levels.

plain**
[plein]

a. 소박한, 꾸미지 않은; (보거나 이해하기에) 분명한
A plain object, surface, or fabric is entirely in one colour and has no pattern, design, or writing on it.

figure out 복습

idiom (생각한 끝에) ~을 이해하다; (양·비용을) 계산하다
If you figure out someone or something, you come to understand them by thinking carefully.

come on 복습

idiom (독촉·설득·격려의 의미로) 자 어서, 빨리; 등장하다, 시작하다
You say 'come on' to encourage someone to do something, for example, to hurry.

shake a leg

idiom 빨리빨리 움직여라
If you say 'shake a leg' to someone, you tell them to hurry or act more quickly.

get the lead out

idiom 서두르다, 행동을 개시하다
If you say 'get the lead out' to someone, you ask them to hurry or move faster.

freckle
[frekl]

n. 주근깨
Freckles are small light brown spots on someone's skin, especially on their face.

cover 복습
[kʌ́vər]

v. (감추거나 보호하기 위해) 씌우다, 가리다, 덮다; 다루다, 포함시키다; n. 덮개
If you cover something, you place something else over it in order to protect it, hide it, or close it.

rich***
[riʧ]

a. 부유한, 돈 많은, 부자인; 풍부한, 풍성한
A rich person has a lot of money or valuable possessions.

aunt**
[ænt]

n. 고모, 이모, (외)숙모
Someone's aunt is the sister of their mother or father, or the wife of their uncle.

trade***
[treid]

v. 주고받다, 교환하다, 맞바꾸다; 거래하다; n. 거래, 교역, 무역
If someone trades one thing for another or if two people trade things, they agree to exchange one thing for the other thing.

spin**
[spin]

v. (spun-spun) (빙빙) 돌다, 회전하다; 돌리다, 회전시키다; n. 회전, 돌기
If something spins or if you spin it, it turns quickly around a central point.

opposite**
[ápəzit]

a. (정)반대의; 건너편의; 맞은편의
Opposite is used to describe things of the same kind which are completely different in a particular way.

dizzy*
[dízi]

a. 어지러운
If you feel dizzy, you feel that you are losing your balance and are about to fall.

race^{복습}
[reis]

v. 급히 가다; 경주하다, 경쟁하다; n. 경주, 달리기 (시합); 경쟁; 인종, 종족
If you race somewhere, you go there as quickly as possible.

announce^{복습}
[ənáuns]

v. 발표하다, 알리다; (공공장소에서) 방송으로 알리다
If you announce something, you tell people about it publicly or officially.

howdy
[háudi]

int. 안녕(만났을 때 하는 인사)
'Howdy' is an informal way of saying 'Hello.'

turn out^{복습}

idiom ~인 것으로 드러나다; 모습을 드러내다; (전기·난방기를) 끄다
If it turns out that something is the case, it is discovered or proved that it is the case.

eventually**
[ivénʧuəli]

ad. 결국, 마침내
Eventually means at the end of a situation or process or as the final result of it.

difficulty**
[dífikʌlti]

n. 어려움, 곤경, 장애
If you have difficulty doing something, you are not able to do it easily.

absolute^{복습}
[ǽbsəlùːt]

a. 완전한, 완벽한; 확실한 (absolutely ad. 틀림없이; 극도로, 굉장히)
You use absolute to emphasize something that you are saying.

Chapters 29 & 30

1. What did Stephen do for Mrs. Jewls' Halloween party?
   A. He came to school on Sunday.
   B. He dressed up as a goblin.
   C. He brought candy for all of the children in class.
   D. He brought cookies that looked like an orange witch with a black hat.

2. Why did Mrs. Gorf say she came to class?
   A. She came to give them candy on Halloween.
   B. She came to give them apples on Halloween.
   C. She came to make them celebrate Halloween.
   D. She came to get even with them all.

3. Why did Stephen run up to Mrs. Goff and hug her?
   A. Mrs. Gorf said that they celebrated Halloween on the Friday before.
   B. Mrs. Gorf said that she liked Stephen's costume.
   C. Mrs. Gorf said that she would save Stephen.
   D. Mrs. Gorf came to class in a costume.

4. Why did the children call Stephen a hero?
   A. He had answered hard math questions.
   B. He had made Mrs. Gorf disappear.
   C. He had come to school dressed like a hero.
   D. He had made them celebrate Halloween.

5. Why did Louis not allow children outside during the blizzard?

A. He was afraid that the children would freeze and catch colds.

B. He was afraid that the children would get lost in the snow.

C. He was afraid that the children would have too much fun.

D. He was afraid that the children would leave school and just go home.

6. How did Louis entertain the children?

A. He told them a story.

B. He showed them all a movie.

C. He told them a funny joke

D. He brought sports equipment to each classroom.

7. How did Mrs. Jewls feel about the story that Louis told the children?

A. She thought it was stupid.

B. She thought it was funny.

C. She thought it was like a fairy tale.

D. She thought it taught the truth to the children.

Check Your Reading Speed

1분에 몇 단어를 읽는지 리딩 속도를 측정해보세요.

$$\frac{690 \text{ words}}{\text{reading time (} \quad \text{) sec}} \times 60 = (\quad) \text{ WPM}$$

Build Your Vocabulary

dress up

idiom 변장을 하다
If you dress up, you dress in a special costume for fun or as part of an entertainment.

goblin
[gáblin]

n. 도깨비
In fairy stories, a goblin is a small, ugly creature which usually enjoys causing trouble.

unfortunate*
[ʌnfɔ́:rtʃənət]

a. 운이 없는, 불운한, 불행한 (unfortunately ad. 불행하게도, 유감스럽게도)
You can use unfortunately to introduce or refer to a statement when you consider that it is sad or disappointing, or when you want to express regret.

dumb^{복습}
[dʌm]

a. 멍청한, 바보 같은; 벙어리의, 말을 못 하는
If you call a person dumb, you mean that they are stupid or foolish.

costume*
[kástju:m]

n. 의상, 복장
A costume is a set of clothes worn in order to look like someone or something else, especially for a party or as part of an entertainment.

witch*
[witʃ]

n. 마녀
In fairy stories, a witch is a woman, usually an old woman, who has evil magic powers.

fool*

n. 바보; v. 속이다, 기만하다
If you call someone a fool, you are indicating that you think they are not at all sensible and show a lack of good judgment.

last**
[læst]

v. (특정한 시간 동안) 계속되다; ad. 맨 끝에, 마지막에
If an event, situation, or problem lasts for a particular length of time, it continues to exist or happen for that length of time.

spend^{복습}
[spend]

v. (시간을) 보내다; (돈을) 쓰다
If you spend time or energy doing something, you use your time or effort doing it.

suit**
[su:t]

n. (특정한 활동 때 입는) 옷[복]; 정장; v. (~에게) 괜찮다; 어울리다
A particular type of suit is a piece of clothing that you wear for a particular activity.

arithmetic^{복습}
[əríθmətik]

n. 산수, 연산; 산술, 계산
Arithmetic is the part of mathematics that is concerned with the addition, subtraction, multiplication, and division of numbers.

108

blackboard^{복습}
[blǽkbɔ̀:rd]

n. 칠판
A blackboard is a dark-colored board that you can write on with chalk.

equal^{복습}
[í:kwəl]

v. (수·양·가치 등이) 같다, ~이다; a. (수·양·가치 등이) 동일한; 동등한, 평등한
If something equals a particular number or amount, it is the same as that amount or the equivalent of that amount.

useless^{**}
[júːslis]

a. 소용없는, 쓸모없는
If something is useless, it does not achieve anything helpful or good.

matter^{복습}
[mǽtər]

n. 문제; 관건; 일, 사안; v. 중요하다; 문제되다
You use no matter in expressions such as 'no matter how' and 'no matter what' to say that something is true or happens in all circumstances.

scream^{복습}
[skri:m]

v. 비명을 지르다, 괴성을 지르다; n. 비명, 절규
When someone screams, they make a very loud, high-pitched cry, because they are in pain or are very frightened.

chalk^{복습}
[ʧɔ:k]

n. 분필
Chalk is a small piece of soft white rock, used for writing or drawing with.

turn into^{복습}

idiom (~에서) ~이 되다, ~으로 변하다
To turn or be turned into something means to become that thing.

squiggle
[skwigl]

v. 비틀어지다, 꿈틀거리다; n. 구불구불한 선
If something squiggles, it moves back and forth with quick irregular motions.

worm^{**}
[wəːrm]

n. 벌레
A worm is a small animal with a long thin body, no bones and no legs.

light up^{복습}

idiom 빛나게 만들다; (얼굴이) 환해지다
If something lights up, it becomes bright or shiny.

screen^{**}
[skri:n]

n. (영화의) 화면, 스크린; (텔레비전·컴퓨터) 화면; v. 가리다, 차단하다
A screen is a flat vertical surface on which pictures or words are shown.

tongue^{복습}
[tʌŋ]

n. 혀; 언어; 말버릇, 말씨
Your tongue is the soft movable part inside your mouth which you use for tasting, eating, and speaking.

pointed^{복습}
[pɔ́intid]

a. (끝이) 뾰족한; (말 등이) 날카로운
Something that is pointed has a point at one end.

fingernail[*]
[fíŋgərnèil]

n. 손톱
Your fingernails are the thin hard areas at the end of each of your fingers.

trick^{복습}
[trik]

n. 속임수; v. 속이다, 속임수를 쓰다
A trick is an action that is intended to deceive someone.

treat^{복습}
[tri:t]

n. (대접하는) 특별한 것, 대접, 한턱; v. (특정한 태도로) 대하다; 여기다, 치부하다
If you give someone a treat, you buy or arrange something special for them which they will enjoy.

rotten^{복습}
[ratn]

a. 형편없는, 끔찍한; 썩은, 부패한
If you describe someone as rotten, you are insulting them or criticizing them because you think that they are very unpleasant or unkind.

get even with

idiom ~에 앙갚음하다, 복수하다
If you get even with someone, you cause them the same amount of trouble or harm as they have caused you.

reunion[*]
[rìːjúːnjən]

n. (오랫동안 못 본 사람들의 친목) 모임, 동창회
A reunion is a party attended by members of the same family, school, or other group who have not seen each other for a long time.

fall on

idiom (날짜가) ~이다
If a celebration or other special event falls on a particular day or date, it happens to be on that day or date.

celebrate^{**}
[séləbrèit]

v. 기념하다, 축하하다
If you celebrate, you do something enjoyable because of a special occasion.

leap[*]
[li:p]

v. (높이·길게) 뛰다, 뛰어오르다; n. 높이 뛰기, 도약
If you leap, you jump high in the air or jump a long distance.

prove^{복습}
[pru:v]

v. 입증하다, 증명하다; (~임이) 드러나다
If you prove that something is true, you show by means of argument or evidence that it is definitely true.

gasp^{복습}
[gæsp]

v. 숨이 턱 막히다, 헉 하고 숨을 쉬다; n. (숨이 막히는 듯) 헉 하는 소리를 냄
When you gasp, you take a short quick breath through your mouth, especially when you are surprised, shocked, or in pain.

wash up

idiom 세수를 하다; 설거지를 하다
If you wash up, you wash your hands and face.

Check Your Reading Speed

1분에 몇 단어를 읽는지 리딩 속도를 측정해보세요.

$$\frac{670 \text{ words}}{\text{reading time ( ) sec}} \times 60 = (\text{) WPM}$$

Build Your Vocabulary

mustache^{복습}
[mʌ́stæʃ]

n. 콧수염
A man's mustache is the hair that grows on his upper lip.

yard^{복습}
[ja:rd]

n. (학교의) 운동장; 마당, 뜰; 정원
A yard is a flat area of concrete or stone that is next to a building and often has a wall around it.

recess^{복습}
[risés]

n. (학교의) 쉬는 시간; (의회·위원회 등의) 휴회 기간
A recess is a break between classes at a school.

blizzard
[blízərd]

n. 눈보라
A blizzard is a very bad snowstorm with strong winds.

lunchroom^{복습}
[lʌ́nʧru:m]

n. (학교·회사 등의) 구내식당
A lunchroom is the room in a school or company where you buy and eat your lunch.

tuna
[tjú:nə]

n. 참치, 참다랑어
Tuna or tuna fish are large fish that live in warm seas and are caught for food.

bore*
[bɔ:r]

v. 지루하게 하다 (bored a. 지루해하는)
If you are bored, you feel tired and impatient because you have lost interest in something or because you have nothing to do.

entertain*
[èntərtéin]

v. 즐겁게 해 주다; (집에서 손님을) 접대하다
If a performer, performance, or activity entertains you, it amuses you, interests you, or gives you pleasure.

behavior**
[bihéivjər]

n. 처신, 행위, 행동 (be on one's best behavior idiom 얌전하게 굴다)
If someone is on their best behavior, they are trying very hard to behave well.

boo
[bu:]

v. (우우하고) 야유하다; n. 야유
If you boo a speaker or performer, you shout 'boo' or make other loud sounds to indicate that you do not like them, their opinions, or their performance.

warn^{복습}
[wɔ:rn]

v. 경고하다, 주의를 주다, 조심하라고 하다
If you warn someone not to do something, you advise them not to do it so that they can avoid possible danger or punishment.

dirt**
[də:rt]

n. 흙; 먼지, 때
You can refer to the earth on the ground as dirt, especially when it is dusty.

ought to ^{복습}

idiom ~할 필요가 있다; ~해야 한다; ~일 것이다
You use ought to when saying that you think it is a good idea and important for you or someone else to do a particular thing, especially when giving or asking for advice or opinions.

confuse ^{복습}
[kənfjúːz]

v. (사람을) 혼란시키다; (주제를) 혼란스럽게 만들다
(confused a. 혼란스러워 하는)
If you are confused, you do not know exactly what is happening or what to do.

story ^{복습}
[stɔ́ːri]

① n. (건물의) 층 ② n. 이야기
A story of a building is one of its different levels, which is situated above or below other levels.

silly ^{복습}
[síli]

a. 어리석은, 바보 같은; n. 바보
If you say that someone or something is silly, you mean that they are foolish, childish, or ridiculous.

assure*
[əʃúər]

v. 장담하다, 확언하다; 확인하다
If you assure someone that something is true or will happen, you tell them that it is definitely true or will definitely happen, often in order to make them less worried.

demand ^{복습}
[dimǽnd]

v. 요구하다; 강력히 묻다, 따지다; n. 요구 (사항); 수요
If you demand something such as information or action, you ask for it in a very forceful way.

turn into ^{복습}

idiom (~에서) ~이 되다, ~으로 변하다
To turn or be turned into something means to become that thing.

raincoat ^{복습}
[réinkòut]

n. 비옷
A raincoat is a waterproof coat.

tuxedo
[tʌksíːdou]

n. 턱시도, (남자용) 예복
A tuxedo is a black or white jacket worn by men for formal social events.

no wonder

idiom 당연하다!; ~은 (별로) 놀랄 일이 아니다, ~하는 것도 당연하다
If you say 'no wonder,' you mean that something is not surprising.

trade ^{복습}
[treid]

v. 주고받다, 교환하다, 맞바꾸다; 거래하다; n. 거래, 교역, 무역
If someone trades one thing for another or if two people trade things, they agree to exchange one thing for the other thing.

upside down ^{복습}
[ápsàid dáun]

ad. (아래위가) 거꾸로
If something has been moved upside down, it has been turned round so that the part that is usually lowest is above the part that is usually highest.

mosquito ^{복습}
[məskíːtou]

n. 모기
Mosquitos are small flying insects which bite people and animals in order to suck their blood.

bite ^{복습}
[bait]

n. (짐승·곤충에게) 물린 상처; 물기; 한 입 (베어 문 조각); v. 물다, 베어 물다
A bite is an injury or a mark on your body where an animal, snake, or small insect has bitten you.

count 복습
[kaunt]

v. 수를 세다; 계산에 넣다; 중요하다; n. 셈, 계산
When you count, you say all the numbers one after another up to a particular number.

equal 복습
[íːkwəl]

v. (수·양·가치 등이) 같다, ~이다; a. (수·양·가치 등이) 동일한; 동등한, 평등한
If something equals a particular number or amount, it is the same as that amount or the equivalent of that amount.

horrible 복습
[hɔ́ːrəbl]

a. 지긋지긋한, 끔찍한; 소름 끼치는, 무시무시한
Horrible is used to emphasize how bad something is.

flavor 복습
[fléivər]

v. 맛을 더하다; n. (음식·술의) 맛 (flavored a. ~맛이 나는)
If you flavor food or drink, you add something to it to give it a particular taste.

hush[*]
[hʌʃ]

n. 침묵, 고요; v. ~을 조용히 시키다
You say there is a hush in a place when everything is quiet and peaceful, or suddenly becomes quiet.

scare 복습
[skɛər]

v. 겁주다, 놀라게 하다 (scared a. 무서워하는, 겁먹은)
If you are scared of someone or something, you are frightened of them.

go in for

idiom ~에 관심이 있다; (시험에) 응시하다; (대회에) 참가하다
If you go in for something, you like it and regularly use or do it.

fairy tale
[fέəri tèil]

n. 동화
A fairy tale is a story for children involving magical events and imaginary creatures.

수고하셨습니다!

드디어 끝까지 다 읽으셨군요! 축하드립니다! 여러분은 이 책을 통해 총 20,395개의 단어를 읽으셨고, 800개 이상의 어휘와 표현들을 익히셨습니다. 이 책에 나온 어휘는 다른 원서를 읽을 때에도 빈번히 만날 수 있는 필수 어휘들입니다. 이 책을 읽었던 경험은 비슷한 수준의 다른 원서들을 읽을 때 큰 도움이 될 것입니다.

이제 자신의 상황에 맞게 원서를 반복해서 읽거나, 오디오북을 들어 볼 수 있습니다. 혹은 비슷한 수준의 다른 원서를 찾아 읽는 것도 좋습니다. 일단 원서를 완독한 뒤에 어떻게 계속 영어 공부를 이어갈 수 있을지, 도움말을 꼼꼼히 살펴보고 각자 상황에 맞게 적용해 보세요!

리딩(Reading)을 확실하게 다지고 싶다면? 반복해서 읽어 보세요!

리딩 실력을 탄탄하게 다지고 싶다면, 같은 원서를 2~3번 반복해서 읽을 것을 권합니다. 같은 책을 여러 번 읽으면 지루할 것 같지만, 꼭 그렇지도 않습니다. 반복해서 읽을 때 처음과 주안점을 다르게 두면, 전혀 다른 느낌으로 재미있게 읽을 수 있습니다.

처음 원서를 읽을 때는 생소한 단어들과 스토리로 인해 읽으면서 곧바로 이해하기가 매우 힘들 수 있습니다. 전체 맥락을 잡고 읽어도 약간 버거운 느낌이지요. 하지만 반복해서 읽기 시작하면 달라집니다. 일단 내용을 파악한 상황이기 때문에 문장 구조나 어휘의 활용에 더 집중하게 되고, 조금 더 깊이 있게 읽을 수 있습니다. 좋은 표현과 문장을 수집하고 메모할 만한 여유도 생기게 되지요. 어휘도 많이 익숙해졌기 때문에 리딩 속도에도 탄력이 붙습니다. 처음 읽을 때는 '내용'에서 재미를 느꼈다면, 반복해서 읽을 때에는 '영어'에서 재미를 느끼게 되는 것입니다. 따라서 리딩 실력을 더욱 확고하게 다지고자 한다면, 같은 책을 2~3회 정도 반복해서 읽을 것을 권해 드립니다.

리스닝(Listening) 실력을 늘리고 싶다면?
귀를 통해서 읽어 보세요!

많은 영어 학습자들이 '리스닝이 안 돼서 문제'라고 한탄합니다. 그리고 리스닝 실력을 늘리는 방법으로 무슨 뜻인지 몰라도 반복해서 듣는 '무작정 듣기'를 선택합니다. 하지만 뜻도 모르면서 무작정 듣는 일에는 엄청난 인내력이 필요합니다. 그래서 대부분 며칠 시도하다가 포기해 버리고 말지요.

따라서 모르는 내용을 무작정 듣는 것보다는 어느 정도 알고 있는 내용을 반복해서 듣는 것이 더 효과적인 듣기 방법입니다. 그리고 이런 방식의 듣기에 활용할 수 있는 가장 좋은 교재가 오디오북입니다.

리스닝 실력을 향상하고 싶다면, 이 책에서 제공하는 오디오북을 이용해서 듣는 연습을 해 보세요. 활용법은 간단합니다. 일단 책을 한 번 완독했다면, 오디오북을 통해 다시 들어 보는 것입니다. 휴대 기기에 넣어 시간이 날 때 틈틈이 듣는 것도 좋고, 책상에 앉아 눈으로는 텍스트를 보며 귀로 읽는 것도 좋습니다. 이미 읽었던 내용이라 이해하기가 훨씬 수월하고, 애매했던 발음들도 자연스럽게 교정할 수 있습니다. 또 성우의 목소리 연기를 듣다 보면 내용이 더욱 생동감 있게 다가와 이해도가 높아지는 효과도 거둘 수 있습니다.

반대로 듣기에 자신 있는 사람이라면, 책을 읽기 전에 처음부터 오디오북을 먼저 듣는 것도 좋은 방법입니다. 귀를 통해 책을 쭉 읽어 보고, 이후에 다시 눈으로 책을 읽으면서 잘 들리지 않았던 부분을 보충하는 것이지요.

중요한 것은 내용을 따라가면서, 내용에 푹 빠져서 반복해 들어야 한다는 것입니다. 이렇게 연습을 반복해서 눈으로 읽지 않은 책이라도 '귀를 통해' 읽을 수 있을 정도가 되면, 리스닝으로 고생하는 일은 거의 없을 것입니다.

이 책은 저자 루이스 새커가 직접 읽은
오디오북을 기본으로 제공하고 있습니다.
오디오북은 MP3 파일로 제공되므로
컴퓨터 또는 휴대 기기에 옮겨서 사용하시면 됩니다.
혹시 오디오북에 이상이 있을 경우
help@ltinc.net으로 메일을 주시면
안내를 받으실 수 있습니다.

스피킹(Speaking)이 고민이라면? 소리 내어 읽어 보세요!

스피킹 역시 많은 학습자들이 고민하는 부분입니다. 스피킹이 고민이라면, 원서를 큰 소리로 읽는 낭독 훈련(Voice Reading)을 해 보세요!

'소리 내어 읽는 것이 말하기에 정말로 도움이 될까?'라고 의아한 생각이 들 수도 있습니다. 하지만 인간의 두뇌 입장에서 봤을 때, 성대 구조를 활용해서 '발화'한다는 점에서는 소리 내어 읽기와 말하기에 큰 차이가 없다고 합니다. 소리 내어 읽는 것은 '타인의 생각'을 전달하고, 직접 말하는 것은 '자신의 생각'을 전달한다는 차이가 있을 뿐, 머릿속에서 문장을 처리하고 조음기관(혀와 성대 등)을 움직여 의미를 만든다는 점에서 같은 과정인 것이지요. 따라서 소리 내어 읽는 연습을 꾸준히 하는 것은 스피킹 연습에 큰 도움이 됩니다.

소리 내어 읽기를 하는 방법은 간단합니다. 일단 오디오북을 들으면서 성우의 목소리를 최대한 따라 하며 같이 읽어 보세요. 발음뿐 아니라 억양, 어조, 느낌까지 완벽히 따라 한다고 생각하면서 소리 내어 읽습니다. 따라 읽는 것이 조금 익숙해지면, 옆의 누군가에게 이 책을 읽어 준다는 생각으로 소리 내어 계속 읽어 나갑니다. 한 번 눈과 귀로 읽었던 책이기 때문에 보다 수월하게 진행할 수 있고, 자연스럽게 어휘와 표현을 복습하는 효과도 거두게 됩니다. 또 이렇게 소리 내어 읽은 것을 녹음해서 들어 보면 스스로에게도 좋은 피드백이 됩니다.

최근 말하기가 강조되면서 소리 내어 읽기가 크게 각광을 받고 있기는 하지만, 그렇다고 소리 내어 읽기가 무조건 좋은 것만은 아닙니다. 책을 소리 내어 읽다 보면, 무의식적으로 속으로 발음을 하는 습관을 가지게 되어 리딩 속도 자체는 오히려 크게 떨어지는 현상이 발생할 수 있습니다. 따라서 빠른 리딩 속도가 중요한 수험생이나 상위권 학습자들에게는 소리 내어 읽기가 적절하지 않은 방법입니다. 효과가 좋다는 말만 믿고 무턱대고 따라 하기보다는 자신의 필요에 맞게 우선순위를 정하고 원서를 활용하는 것이 좋습니다.

라이팅(Writing)까지 욕심이 난다면? 요약하는 연습을 해 보세요!

원서를 라이팅 연습에 직접적으로 활용하는 데에는 한계가 있지만, 적절히 활용하면 원서도 유용한 라이팅 자료가 될 수 있습니다.

특히 책을 읽고 그 내용을 요약하는 연습은 큰 도움이 됩니다. 요약 훈련의 방식도 간단합니다. 원서를 읽고 그날 읽은 분량만큼 혹은 책을 다 읽고 전체 내용을 기반으로, 책 내용을 한번 요약하고 나의 느낌을 영어로 적어 보는 것입니다.

이때 그 책에 나왔던 단어와 표현을 최대한 활용하여 요약하는 것이 중요합니다. 영어 표현력은 결국 얼마나 다양한 어휘로 많은 표현을 해 보았느냐가 좌우하게 됩니다. 이런 면에서 내가 읽은 책을, 그 책에 나온 문장과 어휘로 다시 표현해 보는 것은 매우 효율적인 방법입니다. 책에 나온 어휘와 표현을 단순히 읽고 무슨 말인지 아는 정도가 아니라, 실제로 직접 활용해서 쓸 수 있을 만큼 확실하게 익히게 되는 것이지요. 여기에 첨삭까지 받을 수 있는 방법이 있다면 금상첨화입니다.

이러한 '표현하기' 연습은 스피킹 훈련에도 그대로 적용될 수 있습니다. 책을 읽고 그 내용을 3분 안에 다른 사람에게 영어로 말하는 연습을 해 보세요. 순발력과 표현력을 기르는 좋은 훈련이 될 것입니다.

꾸준히 원서를 읽고 싶다면? 뉴베리 수상작을 계속 읽어 보세요!

뉴베리 상이 세계 최고 권위의 아동 문학상인 만큼, 그 수상작들은 확실히 완성도를 검증받은 작품이라고 할 수 있습니다. 특히 '쉬운 어휘로 쓰인 깊이 있는 문장'으로 이루어졌다는 점이 영어 학습자들에게 큰 호응을 얻고 있습니다. 이렇게 '검증된 원서'를 꾸준히 읽는 것은 영어 실력 향상에 큰 도움이 됩니다.

아래에 수준별로 제시된 뉴베리 수상작 목록을 보며 적절한 책들을 찾아 계속 읽어 보세요. 꼭 뉴베리 수상작이 아니더라도 마음에 드는 작가의 다른 책을 읽어 보는 것 또한 아주 좋은 방법입니다.

• 영어 초보자도 쉽게 읽을 만한 아주 쉬운 수준. 소리 내어 읽기에도 아주 적합.
Sarah, Plain and Tall*(Medal, 8,331단어), The Hundred Penny Box (Honor, 5,878단어), The Hundred Dresses*(Honor, 7,329단어), My Father's Dragon (Honor, 7,682단어), 26 Fairmount Avenue (Honor, 6,737단어)

• 중·고등학생 정도 영어 학습자라면 쉽게 읽을 수 있는 수준. 소리 내어 읽기에도 비교적 적합한 편.

Because of Winn-Dixie*(Honor, 22,123단어), What Jamie Saw (Honor, 17,203단어), Charlotte's Web (Honor, 31,938단어), Dear Mr. Henshaw (Medal, 18,145단어), Missing May (Medal, 17,509단어)

• 대학생 정도 영어 학습자라면 무난한 수준. 소리 내어 읽기에는 적합하지 않음.

Number The Stars*(Medal, 27,197단어), A Single Shard (Medal, 33,726단어), The Tale of Despereaux*(Medal, 32,375단어), Hatchet*(Medal, 42,328단어), Bridge to Terabithia (Medal, 32,888단어), A Fine White Dust (Honor, 19,022단어), Jennifer, Hecate, Macbeth, William McKinley and Me, Elizabeth (Honor, 23,266단어)

• 원서 완독 경험을 가진 학습자에게 적절한 수준. 소리 내어 읽기에는 적합하지 않음.

The Giver*(Medal, 43,617단어), From the Mixed-Up Files of Mrs. Basil E. Frankweiler (Medal, 30,906단어), The View from Saturday (Medal, 42,685단어), Holes*(Medal, 47,079단어), Criss Cross (Medal, 48,221단어), Walk Two Moons (Medal, 59,400단어), The Graveyard Book (Medal, 67,380단어)

뉴베리 수상작과 뉴베리 수상 작가의 좋은 작품을 엄선한 「뉴베리 컬렉션」에도 위 목록에 있는 도서 중 상당수가 포함될 예정입니다.

★ 「뉴베리 컬렉션」으로 이미 출간된 도서

어떤 책들이 출간되었는지 확인하려면, 지금 인터넷 서점에서
뉴베리 컬렉션을 검색해 보세요.

뉴베리 수상작을 동영상 강의로 만나 보세요!

영어원서 전문 동영상 강의 사이트 영서당(yseodang.com)에서는 뉴베리 컬렉션 『Wayside School』 시리즈, 『Holes』, 『Because of Winn-Dixie』, 『The Miraculous Journey of Edward Tulane』 등의 동영상 강의를 제공하고 있습니다. 뉴베리 수상작이라는 최고의 영어 교재와 EBS 출신 인기 강사가 만난 명강의! 지금 사이트를 방문해서 무료 샘플 강의를 들어 보세요!

'스피드 리딩 카페'를 통해 원서 읽기 습관을 길러 보세요!

일상에서 영어를 한마디도 쓰지 않는 비영어권 국가에서 살고 있는 우리가 영어 환경에 가장 쉽고, 편하고, 부담 없이 노출되는 방법은 바로 '영어원서 읽기'입니다. 언제 어디서든 원서를 붙잡고 읽기만 하면 곧바로 영어를 접하는 환경이 만들어지기 때문이지요. 하루에 20분씩만 꾸준히 읽는다면, 1년에 무려 120시간 동안 영어에 노출될 수 있습니다. 이러한 이유 때문에 영어 교육 전문가들이 영어원서 읽기를 추천하는 것이지요.

하지만 원서 읽기가 좋다는 것을 알아도 막상 꾸준히 읽는 것은 쉽지 않습니다. 그럴 때에는 13만 명 이상의 회원을 보유한 국내 최대 원서 읽기 동호회 〈스피드 리딩 카페〉(cafe.naver. com/readingtc)를 방문해 보세요.

원서별로 정리된 무료 PDF 단어장과 수준별 추천 원서 목록 등 유용한 자료는 물론, 뉴베리 수상작을 포함한 다양한 원서의 리뷰를 무료로 확인할 수 있습니다. 특히 함께 모여서 원서를 읽는 '북클럽'은 중간에 포기하지 않고 원서를 끝까지 읽는 습관을 기르는 데 큰 도움이 될 것입니다.

Introduction and Chapter 1

1. B   It was supposed to be only one story high, with thirty classrooms all in a row.

2. C   Instead it is thirty stories high, with one classroom on each story.

3. B   The children at Wayside like having a sideways school. They have an extra-large playground.

4. D   One day Mrs Gorf caught Joe copying John's paper. She wiggled her ears—first her right one, then her left—stuck out her tongue, and turned Joe into an apple. Then she turned John into an apple for letting Joe cheat.

5. D   Louis, the yard teacher, walked into the classroom. He had missed the children at recess. He had heard that Mrs. Gorf was a mean teacher. So he came up to investigate. He saw the twelve apples on Mrs. Gorf's desk. "I must be wrong," he thought. "She must be a good teacher if so many children bring her apples." He walked back down to the playground.

6. A   "No!" screamed Mrs. Gorf. "I'll turn you back into apples." She wiggled her ears—first her right one, then her left—and stuck out her tongue. But Jenny held up a mirror, and Mrs. Gorf turned herself into an apple.

7. C   "Boy, am I hungry," said Louis. "I don't think Mrs. Gorf would mind if I ate this apple. After all, she always has so many."

Chapters 2 & 3

1. A   The children on the thirtieth story were scared. They had never told anybody what had happened to Mrs. Gorf. They hadn't had a teacher for three days. They were afraid of what their new teacher would be like. They had heard she'd be a terribly nice teacher. They had never had a nice teacher. They were terribly afraid of nice teachers.

2. C   Mrs. Jewls looked at the children. They were horribly cute. In fact, they were much too cute to be children. "I don't believe it," said Mrs. Jewls. "It's a room full of monkeys!"

3. B   Jason tapped Todd on the shoulder. He said, "Do you want to know something? I liked it better when she thought we were monkeys." "I know," said Todd. "I guess now it means she won't bring me a banana."

4. D   "Joe, you are going to have to learn how to count," said Mrs. Jewls.

5. C   "This doesn't make any sense," said Joe. "When I count the wrong way I get the right answer, and when I count right I get the wrong answer."

6. A   "School just speeds things up," said Mrs. Jewls. "Without school it might take another seventy years before you wake up and are able to count."

7. B   When Joe woke up the next day, he knew how to count. He had fifty five thousand and six hairs on his head. They were all curly.

Chapters 4 & 5

1. D   Sharie had long eyelashes. She weighed only forty-nine pounds. She always wore a big red and blue overcoat with a hood.

2. A   She sat next to the window in Mrs. Jewls's class. She spent a lot of time just staring out the window. Mrs. Jewls didn't mind. Mrs. Jewls said that a lot of people learn best when they stare out a window. Sharie often fell asleep in class. Mrs. Jewls didn't mind that, either. She said that a lot of people do their best learning when they are asleep.

3. B   After she had fallen ten stories, Sharie woke up. She looked around. She was confused. She wasn't in Mrs. Jewls's class, and she wasn't at home in bed. She couldn't figure out where she was. She yawned, pulled the hood back over her eyes, and went back to sleep. By that time she had fallen another ten stories.

4. D   "Todd," she said, "you know better than to talk in class. You must learn to work quietly, like the other children." She wrote his name on the blackboard under the word DISCIPLINE.

5. C   A child was given three chances in Mrs. Jewls's class. The first time he did something wrong, Mrs. Jewls wrote his name on the blackboard under the word DISCIPLINE. The second time he did something wrong, she put a check next to his name. And the third time he did something wrong, she circled his name.

6. B   Todd really tried to be good. He knew that if he talked one more time, Mrs. Jewls would circle his name. Then he'd have to go home early, at twelve o'clock, on the kindergarten bus, just as he had the day before and the day before that. In fact, there hadn't been a day since Mrs. Jewls took over the class that she didn't send Todd home early. She said she did it for his own good. The other children went home at two o'clock.

7. A   Todd's eyes lit up. "We sure do," he said. "We have knowledge." He grabbed

Joy's workbook and gave it to the robbers. "Knowledge is much more valuable than money."

Chapters 6 & 7

1. C   Bebe was a girl with short brown hair, a little beebee nose, totally tiny toes, and big brown eyes. Her full name was Bebe Gunn. She was the fastest draw in Mrs. Jewls's class.

2. D   Calvin sat next to Bebe. He didn't think he was very good at art. Why, it took him the whole period just to draw one airplane. So instead, he just helped Bebe. He was Bebe's assistant. As soon as Bebe would finish one masterpiece, Calvin would take it from her and set down a clean sheet of paper.

3. A   "No," said Mrs. Jewls. "That isn't how you measure art. It isn't how many pictures you have, but how good the pictures are. Why, a person could spend his whole life just drawing one picture of a cat. In that time I'm sure Bebe could draw a million cats."

4. B   "Calvin," said Mrs. Jewls, "I want you to take this note to Miss Zarves for me."

5. D   As you know, when the builder built Wayside School, he accidentally built it sideways. But he also forgot to build the nineteenth story. He built the eighteenth and the twentieth, but no nineteenth. He said he was very sorry. There was also no Miss Zarves. Miss Zarves taught the class on the nineteenth story. Since there was no nineteenth story, there was no Miss Zarves. And besides that, as if Calvin didn't have enough problems, there was no note. Mrs. Jewls had never given Calvin the note.

6. C   "Thank you very much, Calvin," said Mrs. Jewls. Calvin said, "But I—" Mrs. Jewls interrupted him. "That was a very important note, and I'm glad I was able to count on you."

7. A   "The note was very important," said Mrs. Jewls. "I told Miss Zarves not to meet me for lunch."

Chapters 8 & 9

1. B   "It's a difficult job," said Mrs. Jewls. "But you can do it. You must turn the lights on every morning and turn them off at the end of the day."

2. C   Myron wanted to be the best president ever. But it was such an easy job, he thought, that anybody could do it. When school let out that day, Myron stayed behind. He turned out the lights by flicking the switch down.

3. D   Pugsy lay unconscious in the street. Myron carefully picked her up. He carried her two miles to the vet. Dana cried at his side.

4. A   "It's about time you got here, Myron," said Mrs. Jewls. "We have no lights." "Why didn't somebody else just turn them on?" asked Myron. "Because you're class president," said Mrs. Jewls. "Show Stephen how to work the lights. From now on he will be class president."

5. B   Maurecia got tired of ice cream. By that time her desk was a mess, and everything in it was sticky.

6. D   "This ice cream has no taste," said Maurecia. "It doesn't taste bad, but it doesn't taste good. It doesn't taste like anything at all!"

7. C   This turned out to be a problem. Every once in a while Maurecia would try to take a bite out of Todd's arm in order to get that very special flavor.

Chapters 10 & 11

1. C   Paul had the best seat in Mrs. Jewls's class. He sat in the back of the room. It was the seat that was the farthest away from Mrs. Jewls.

2. A   Paul saw those pigtails, and a terrible urge came over him. He wanted to pull a pigtail. He wanted to wrap his fist around it, feel the hair between his fingers, and just yank.

3. D   "I bet," said Paul. "Just like she didn't mind the last time." "You just didn't pull hard enough," said the pigtail. "Leslie likes us pulled real hard." "Really?" asked Paul. "Cross my heart," said the pigtail, "the harder, the better." "Okay," said Paul. "but if you're lying . . ." "I promise," said the pigtail. Paul grabbed the left pigtail. It felt good in his hand. He pulled as hard as he could.

4. C   In fact, Paul could do this every day. He could pull Leslie's pigtails twice, and then stay out of trouble the rest of the day. There was nothing Leslie could do about it.

5. D   "Oh, no, Mrs. Jewls," said Dana. "I can't do arithmetic. I itch all over. I can't concentrate."

6. B   Mrs. Jewls continued. "We'll just have to turn your mosquito bites into numbers."

7. A   "I'm glad we turned my mosquito bites into numbers instead of letters," said Dana. "I could never spell *mosquito*."

Chapters 12 & 13

1. D   "Mrs. Jewls," Jason called without raising his hand. "Joy is chewing gum in

class!" Joy had the biggest mouth in Mrs. Jewls's class. And it was filled with gum. There was hardly even room for her tongue. "Joy, I'm ashamed of you," said Mrs. Jewls. "I'm afraid I'll have to put your name up on the board."

2. C   "Wait," said Joy. "Mrs. Jewls, if I can get Jason unstuck, do I still have to go home on the kindergarten bus?" "All right," said Mrs. Jewls. "If you can somehow get Jason free, you don't have to go home early."

3. A   Joy stepped up and kissed him on the nose. Jason fell out of the chair and hit his head on the floor.

4. B   Rondi had twenty-two beautiful teeth. Everyone else had twenty-four. Rondi was missing her two front teeth. And those were the most beautiful teeth of all.

5. C   Suddenly, everybody who was sitting near her began to laugh. "What's so funny?" asked Todd. "The joke Rondi didn't tell," said Jason.

6. A   "But, Mrs. Jewls," said Rondi. "I didn't tell a joke." "Yes, I know," said Mrs. Jewls, "but the funniest jokes are the ones that remain untold."

7. B   Rondi screamed. She socked Louis in the stomach, then bit his arm with her missing teeth. And that kind of bite hurts the worst.

Chapters 14 & 15

1. C   It was a horrible, stinky, rainy day. Some rainy days are fun and exciting, but not this one. This one stunk. All the children were wet and wore smelly raincoats. The whole room smelled awful.

2. D   There was one good thing, however. There was a new boy in class. New kids are always fun. Except no one could even tell what the new boy looked like. He was completely covered by his raincoat.

3. C   Dead rats were always trying to sneak into Mrs. Jewls's class. That was the third one she'd caught since September.

4. A   Deedee meant anything besides the yellow ball. There was one yellow ball at Wayside School and Louis was always trying to get rid of it. It didn't bounce, and it never went the way it was kicked.

5. A   So Deedee's problem was to figure out a way to get a green ball, or at least a red ball.

6. B   Just before recess, Deedee smeared the cream cheese and jelly all over her face. Then she stuffed her mouth with nuts and hung the shredded cheese from her nose. When she closed her eyes, she looked just like a dead rat. Todd was in on the plan. "Mrs. Jewls," he called. "There's a dead rat in the classroom." Mrs. Jewls was very put out. "I

124

want that dead rat outside immediately!" When Mrs. Jewls said *immediately*, she meant it. Deedee instantly found herself outside on the playground.

7. D   "Terrific," said Louis. "I always wanted to be best friends with a dead rat."

Chapters 16 & 17

1. A   Mrs. Jewls heard him. She began to write Todd's name on the board under DISCIPLINE, but when she saw D.J.'s smile, she put down the chalk. "Good morning, D.J.," she said. "What are you so happy about?"

2. D   Everyone took one guess. "Have you been swimming?" "Is it your birthday?" "Are you in love?" "Did you get a green ball?" Nobody guessed right.

3. B   "Come on, D.J. You can tell me. Why are you so happy?" D.J. looked up at him. He said, "You need a reason to be sad. You don't need a reason to be happy."

4. C   John had light brown hair and a round head. He was Joe's best friend. John was one of the smartest boys in Mrs. Jewls's class. But he had one problem. He could only read words written upside down.

5. B   "I know I'm right," said Mrs. Jewls. "You are going to have to learn to stand on your head."

6. C   "We'll help you, John," said Mrs. Jewls. "Joe, get off John's head and get me the pillow from under my desk. Nancy, Calvin, come here and give us a hand." Mrs. Jewls took the pillow from Joe and set it on the floor. "All right, John, we'll surround you," she said. "We won't let you fall."

7. A   "Yes, I think so. I feel a little funny. Hey! I can still read the blackboard, and I'm not upside down. I can read right side up now. When I fell, I must have flipped my brain or something."

Chapters 18 & 20

1. C   But Leslie had one problem. She didn't know what to do with her toes. She had ten adorable little toes and nothing to do with them. As far as she could tell, they served no useful purpose.

2. B   During recess, she asked Dana. "Dana, what do you do with your toes?" "I scratch the back of my legs," said Dana. "First I scratch my left leg with my right foot. Then I scratch my right leg with my left foot."

3. A   "Nothing doing," said Leslie. "These toes are sold as a set. It's either all ten for fifty cents or no deal. What am I going to do with just eight toes?"

4. B   "Wait a second," Louis called. "I'll give you a dollar each for your pigtails." Leslie turned around and looked at him with fiery eyes. "Cut my hair!" she exclaimed. "Are you crazy?"

5. C   She doesn't like the people she knows, either. She hates everybody in Mrs. Jewls's class. She did like one member of the class. She liked Sammy. She thought he was funny. Sammy was a dead rat.

6. A   Kathy once had a cat named Skunks. She liked Skunks. But she was afraid that Skunks would run away. "You have nothing to worry about, Kathy," said Mrs. Jewls. "Skunks won't run away. Just be nice to him and feed him and pet him, and he won't run away. He may go out and play, but he'll always come back." "No, you're wrong, Mrs. Jewls," said Kathy. "What do you know! He'll run away." So Kathy kept Skunks locked up in her closet at home. She never let him out and sometimes even forgot to feed him. One day, while Kathy was looking for her other shoe, Skunks ran out of the closet and never came back. "You said he would come back, Mrs. Jewls," said Kathy. "He never came back. You were wrong. I was right." That was why Kathy didn't like Mrs. Jewls.

7. D   But she also has a good reason for not liking you. And she doesn't even know you. Her reason is this. She knows that if you ever met her, you wouldn't like her. You don't like Kathy, do you?

Chapters 21 & 22

1. D   "It isn't your ball," said Louis. "You gave it to me," said Terrence. "I gave it to you to share," said Louis. "If you can't share it, you can't have it."

2. B   "Ron and I will stand everybody!" Louis announced. ... Ron pitched, and Louis played the other eight positions. Twenty minutes later, they finally got three outs. The score was twenty-one to nothing.

3. A   "Hey, now wait a second," said Ron. "Don't go blaming it all on me. You're half the team, too, you know." And with that, he punched Louis in the stomach.

4. B   They were known throughout the school for being fat. Eric Fry sat at this end of the room. Eric Bacon sat in the middle of the room. And Eric Ovens sat at that end of the room. There was a joke around Wayside School that if all three Erics were ever at the same end of the room at the same time, the whole school would tip over.

5. D   Eric Bacon hated jokes like that. That's not surprising. After all, he wasn't even fat. In fact, he was the skinniest kid in Mrs. Jewls's class. But nobody seemed to notice. The other two Erics were fat, and so everyone just thought that all Erics were fat.

6. C   Eric Fry was playing right field. Terrence belted a deep fly to left. Eric Fry

raced all the way across the field after the ball and at the last second dived at it. He caught it in midair on his fingertips, but as he hit the ground the ball squirted loose. "Well, what do you expect from 'Butterfingers,'" said Stephen. And since that time Eric Fry has had the nickname "Butterfingers."

7. C   All three of the Erics had nicknames. It was better that way. Otherwise when someone said, "Hey, Eric," no one knew to whom he was talking. One time all the Erics would answer, and the next time none of them would answer. But when someone said, "Hey, 'Crabapple,'" then Eric Ovens knew they were talking to him. And if someone said, "Hey, 'Butterfingers,'" Eric Fry knew they meant him. And when someone said, "Hey, 'Fat-so,'" Eric Bacon knew that he was being called.

Chapters 23 & 24

1. B   Allison used to say that she knocked Rondi's teeth out. Allison was very pretty, so all the boys in Mrs. Jewls's class teased her, especially Jason. But Allison said, "Leave me alone or I'll knock your teeth out—like I did Rondi's." The boys didn't bother her after that.

2. D   Allison went back inside and up the thirty flights of stairs to Mrs. Jewls's room. The lunch period wasn't over yet, but Allison didn't feel like doing anything else. She had given her food to the lunch teacher, her book to the librarian, and her ball to the yard teacher. She went inside her classroom.

3. C   "You learned that children are really smarter than their teachers," said Mrs. Jewls.

4. D   "Dameon," said Mrs. Jewls, "run downstairs and ask Louis if he'd like to see the movie with us."

5. A   Dameon had missed the movie, but he still could have written something about turtles: "Turtles are too slow." But now he couldn't find his pencil. It just wasn't his day. "What's the matter, Dameon?" asked Mrs. Jewls. "I can't find my pencil," said Dameon.

6. C   "Okay, class," said Mrs. Jewls. "So that we have no more mix-ups, I want everybody to write his name on his pencil."

7. D   Dameon spent the rest of the day trying to write his name on his pencil.

Chapters 25 & 26

1. D   Jenny came to school on the back of her father's motorcycle. She was late. Wayside School began at nine o'clock. It was almost nine-thirty. She kissed her father good-bye and raced up the thirty flights of stairs to Mrs. Jewls's room.

2. C   "Oh, I hope they didn't go on a field trip without me." She looked out the window. Nobody was there, not even Louis.

3. D   "It would seem to me," the man said, "that if a child came to school and nobody was there, she might play games, or walk around, or go home, but certainly not work on spelling."

4. B   "Jenny," the bald man called. Jenny turned slowly around. "Yes?" she whispered. "Next time, don't come to school on a Saturday.

5. A   Terrence was a good athlete but a bad sport.

6. C   "Can I play?" asked Terrence. "No," said Calvin. "You'll just kick the ball over the fence."

7. D   "You heard him, Louis," said Terrence. "Let me have it." "Okay," said Louis. He picked Terrence up and kicked him over the fence.

Chapters 27 & 28

1. C   Joy had forgotten her lunch at home. It was lunchtime. She was hungry.

2. B   Dameon hadn't forgotten his lunch. He had brought a lovely turkey sandwich, a big piece of chocolate cake, and a crisp, red apple. All he needed was a glass of milk. He could get that from Miss Mush. Miss Mush didn't know how to ruin milk. Dameon left his lunch on his desk and went to the end of the milk line.

3. A   "No," said Joy, "not really. Since Dameon didn't get to eat, he can have it." "Thanks a lot!" said Dameon. "You are the greatest!" He ate Joy's lunch, an old bologna sandwich and a dried-up carrot.

4. B   Nancy had big hands and big feet. He didn't like his name. He thought it was a girl's name.

5. C   They were friends for a good reason. He didn't know her name, and she didn't know his. They just called each other "Hey, you," or just plain "You."

6. D   They both spun around one hundred times in opposite directions until they were so dizzy that they fell over. When they stood up, Mac was Nancy and Nancy was Mac.

7. A   Everybody just decided to keep his own name. The children didn't like them, but it made things much easier.

128

Chapters 29 & 30

1. B   Stephen had green hair. He had purple ears and a blue face. He wore his sister's pink dancing shoes and green leotards. The leotards matched his hair. He was all dressed up as a goblin for Mrs. Jewls's Halloween party.

2. D   Mrs. Gorf ran her fingernails across the blackboard. "Trick or treat, you rotten kids," she said. "Now I'll get even with every last one of you. Where's Todd?"

3. A   Stephen leaped up from his seat. "See, I was right," he said. "Today is the day we celebrate it, the Friday before! Mrs. Gorf proved it." He ran up to Mrs. Gorf. "They all laughed at me and made me feel stupid because I was the only one who got dressed up. But they were the ones who were wrong. You and I are right." He put his arms around Mrs. Gorf and hugged her.

4. B   All the children who had laughed at Stephen now called him a hero. But they told him to change out of his stupid costume.

5. C   On June tenth there was a blizzard. Louis was afraid that the children would have too much fun, so nobody was allowed outside.

6. A   Mrs. Jewls continued, "Louis is going to come up and entertain us. He will tell us a story. Now I want you all to be on your best behavior."

7. C   Mrs. Jewls said, "Louis, it was a very entertaining story. But we don't really go in for fairy tales here. I'm trying to teach my class the truth."

SIDEWAYS STORIES FROM WAYSIDE SCHOOL

1판 1쇄	2015년 1월 2일
2판 4쇄	2023년 9월 18일

지은이	Louis Sachar
기획	이수영
책임편집	김보경 정소이
콘텐츠제작및감수	롱테일북스 편집부
저작권	김보경
마케팅	김보미 정경훈

펴낸이	이수영
펴낸곳	롱테일북스
출판등록	제2015-000191호
주소	04033 서울특별시 마포구 양화로 113, 3층 (서교동, 순흥빌딩)
전자메일	help@ltinc.net

ISBN 979-11-91343-01-4 14740